The Great Book of
Dragon
Patterns

by Lora S. Irish

Fox
Chapel Publishing Co. Inc.

1970 Broad Street • East Petersburg, PA 17520 • www.foxchapelpublishing.com

Publisher:	Alan Giagnocavo
Editor:	Ayleen Stellhorn
Desktop Specialist:	Linda L. Eberly, Eberly Designs Inc.
Cover Photography:	Robert Polett
Cover Design:	Timothy Mize

Cover Art: Lora S. Irish (www.classiccarvingpatterns.com), paper cuttings, oil paintings, acrylic paintings, watercolors, woodburnings, needlepoint, airbrushed denim.
Sam Willcox (http://willcoxdesign.com), Intarsia dragon, based on the Dragon Portrait pattern on page 95.
Gary Browning (http://angelfire.com/md2/creativewood/browning.htm), scroll sawed dragons, based on the Celtic Cross Dragons pattern on page 87.

ISBN 1–56523–155–4
Library of Congress Card Number 2001091371

To order your copy of this book,
please remit the cover price
plus $3.00 shipping to:
Fox Chapel Publishing Company
Book Orders
1970 Broad Street
East Petersburg, PA 17520

Or visit us on the web at
www.carvingworld.com

Manufactured in Korea

Lora S. Irish and her husband, Mike, maintain a website featuring a wide variety of patterns. Visit them on the web at www.classiccarvingpatterns.com

Dedication

Dedicated to our son, Kent Shay Irish. His enthusiasm, creative ideas, and zest for this project made the winged beasts in "The Great Book of Dragon Patterns" come alive.

Table of Contents

Acknowledgments

Special thanks are extended to Alan Giagnocavo, Ayleen Stellhorn, and Linda Eberly for the excellent work in the editing and design of this manual. The extra touches and attention to the small details are obvious throughout the book.

Robert Polett's fine photography, Sam Willcox's beautiful Intarsia work, and Gary Browning's fine scroll sawing skills have added the final finishing touches.

Introduction

From the earliest creation stories to contemporary fantasy tales, dragons fill the sky. They are wonderful, winged beasts that fight the reluctant hero, raid our livestock herds for food, terrorize our villages, and abduct our first born maiden children. Bright, golden sails block the sun when they take to the heavens, the celestial bodies are eclipsed when they feast upon the stars, and the earth trembles when they return to land. These monstrous animals can be our worst enemies, representing everything evil and vile that we can imagine, or they can become our closest allies, their very lives bounded to ours.

Nothing is certain about dragons, except the fact that they have captured our imaginations since the beginning of time. Greens, reds, blues, blacks, opalescent tones—dragons come in every color under the sun. Two-winged serpents, two-legged worms, four-limbed drakes... The variety of the species is large, each animal different than its cousins.

As artists, we are especially enthralled with the idea of the winged beast. We have used their images to decorate the armor our heroes have taken to battle, to accent the pages of our written texts, and to fill our canvases with open sails and curling tails. With today's resurgence in the popularity of dragons, these beasts have become a favorite theme for both the fine artist and the crafter. Winged Lizards dance across hand-painted T-shirts and Sea Serpents sail oceans created on needlepoint canvases. Dragons are extremely adaptable subjects for any art medium or style.

"Know your subject" is the mantra of artists. Only by understanding and comprehending that which we wish to represent in our art are we able to create images that are both believable and that will have an emotional impact on the viewer. With today's resurgence of the dragon ideology and imagery, it is especially important for us to take a look at dragonkind through the lens of mythology. In this way, we can come to understand the art and symbolism that has gone before us and put those ideas to use in today's works.

This book is meant to be a brief synopsis for the dragon artist, a gathering together of the beasts that have appeared in legends and tales throughout the Western world. We will explore some of the species that have been recorded, look at how their bodies may be constructed, and take a fun look at how our writers of past ages have portrayed these monsters.

Throughout the text, you will find patterns for the classic dragon, including free-form beasts, architectural accents, heraldry designs, and of course, playful characters. As you work through the pages, you will learn how to take these patterns and adapt them to create unique dragons of your own.

In conclusion, this book is meant only as a starting point for the dragon artist. My hope is that within these pages you might find some ideas, some imagery that you may then use to create a world full of winged serpents unlike any seen before.

—Lora S. Irish

Dragon
Art

OR How do I use this book in my artwork?

Artists are constantly looking for new ideas that can be adapted to their work. The dragon patterns within these pages are designed so that you, the artist, can not only use them directly from the pages but also manipulate the designs to better fulfill your needs. So whether you are a scroll saw artist, needle arts designer, or a fine arts oil painter, you will discover that these patterns can easily be adapted to your specialty.

Because the dragon is created from man's imagination, his body shape, adornments, skin texture, color, and even his environment are open to the interruption of the crafter. Many of the physical features can be stretched or compressed to meet the size and area limitations of the media in which you are working.

An example of the simple changes an artist can effect is found in the wood burned mirror. This dragon pattern is displayed on page 113. From the original drawing the dragon's tail has been elongated to encompass the edges on the mirror frame, the wings have been stretched, and the orb has been reduced to fit the working area. With just these few changes the pattern now becomes a mirror dragon design. It is my hope and my intention that these gallery pages will spark many ideas for your creative work.

Intarsia dragon (wood) by Sam Willcox.
Based on "Dragon Portrait," page 95.

Woodburned box with lid,
based on "Ribbed-Back Sample Dragon," page 80.

Airbrushed denim jacket,
based on "Entwined Tail Knots," page 129.

Oil on canvas,
based on "Double-Horned Monarch," page 77.

Scroll sawed fretwork (wood),
by Gary Browning.
Based on "Celtic Cross Dragons," page 87.

Woodburned mirror frame (pyrography),
based on "Wyvern Orb Mirror
Image," page 113.

Airbrushed denim jeans,
based on "Dragon Curl," page 92.

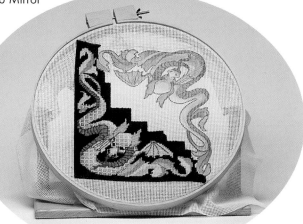

Needlepoint in progress,
based on "Corner Accent Dragons," page 102.

Tole painted shelf,
based on "Fire Heights," page 61.

Watercolor,
based on "Proudly Perched Western," page 138.

Oil on canvas,
based on "Classic Western Dragon," page 107.

Panel Winged Bearded Serpent,
oil on canvas (variation on "Panel Winged Serpent," page 133).

Watercolor,
based on the scale grid-work illustration, page 42.

Oil on canvas,
based on " On the Prowl," page 100.

Cut paper,
based on "Celtic Cross Dragons," page 87.

Fantasy Dragon,
oil on canvas.

Fire Breath,
watercolor.

Tole painted Welcome sign,
based on "Young Fairy Love," page 118.

Cut paper,
based on "Wyvern Mirror," page 98.

Cut paper,
based on "Ocean Crest," page 68.

Hand-painted needlepoint canvas,
based on "Sentinel," page 60.

Well-Guarded Orb,
water color (variation on
"Wyvern Mirror," page 98).

Oil on canvas,
based on "Heart Dragon Mirror Image,"
page 134.

Basic Dragon Traits 2

OR What does a dragon do when it's not fighting heroes?

As artists hoping to make believable renderings of these amazing creatures, it is important to understand the history and lore of the dragon before actually creating our own pictures of the beast. Throughout history the dragon appears in legends, mythologies, and oral traditions as an adversary to mankind. They are more than simple animal characters that appear within the tales. Dragons are used as an element within the myths to symbolize the forces and fears that man must overcome to survive and grow within his world. As mankind grew and developed, his obstacles, fears, and desires changed. So within the myths you will see that the dragon evolves from a simple worm-like creature into the four legged winged beast of today. The dragon comes to be assigned certain physical traits, ecological nooks, and personality characteristics as it changes to meet the needs of the legend.

This chapter explores the basic traits, lifecycle, and characteristics that have been assigned to the dragon. This will help to define the basic environment and setting of your dragon scene.

The Beast's Lair

The earliest legends, those that explain the creation of the heavens and the earth, tell of dragons that occupied the void of the universe. Their great bodies were destined to become the basis for the stars, their flaming breath created the trails from passing comets. These beasts were considered so large that they ate the Sun and the Moon, causing terrifying eclipses, then regurgitated these celestial bodies because they were indigestible.

Soon the dragon moved from the heavens to become a land-dwelling creature. Heavily forested areas were now the homes for dragons, yet even with this move into the woods, the beast was always noted as living near some body of water. A heavily wooded swamp was considered prime territory.

The next domains are noted as being watery areas. Snake-like beasts often took up residency in a nearby fresh-water lake or pond, living much like the modern-day Loch Ness Monster. Lake monsters were seldom seen in their entire form. Long, thin necks, back fins and occasionally a tail tip were all that emerged from their murky homes.

As man began to venture out onto the seas and oceans, dragons began appearing in the legends of the sailors. Many maps created during this period of exploration have notations to warn other sailors of areas that were considered to be infested with Sea Serpents.

It was not until later that dragons took up residence near populated areas, living close enough to man to cause a problem for both species. The Worms of the British Isles are examples of the beasts that made this type of area their home. Curling their massive bodies around small hill mounds or tree groves near the local creek, these great animals settled themselves near human villages and towns.

The Western dragons, the most modern of all dragon species, finally settled in to become cave dwellers. The cave offered excellent protection from their nearby neighbors, man, and allowed the dragons to safely raise their families. Caves that are found along the sides of cliffs are most preferred because the only access to the openings was by wing.

Historically, dragons were solitary creatures, living one to a territory except during the mating season. Western Dragons, however, discovered that safety could be found in large numbers or groups. Family groupings of dragons now become common, with the animals in one cave being the offspring of one Queen. This is the first time that more than one dragon is living within a region or territory.

A Meal Fit for a Dragon

By the time man established his own population with growing towns and cities, the dragons had moved farther

Dragons of later lore made their homes in cliff-side caves, far from the reach of humans.

and farther away from the deep lakes and heavily forested regions. The beast now discovered that though living close to man could be very dangerous, it also provided an abundance of food. The herds of livestock being raised by these small agricultural populations were ideal sources.

Dragons seldom ate people. They did, whenever possible, snack on a tasty oxen or ram or even an occasional boar if the animal could be run to the ground before it gored the hunting dragon. Elephants were a favorite entrée, well worthy of the time and energy involved in catching them. But it is clear through the historical stories that eating a human was only done when either the beast was starving to death, having consumed all other available food sources, or the human had become such a nuisance to the beast that eating him was an act of self defense for the dragon.

There are a few stories that imply that dragons did eat some vegetables, however, it is always noted that the dragons did so only to relieve stomach or intestinal discomforts. Usually it was lettuce or, of all things, broccoli that the dragons used as remedies.

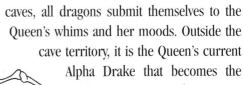

The Dragon's Social Circles

Dragons are divided into two sexes: the male, which can be called a Drake, and the female, which is referred to as a Queen. Extremely little is noted in the earliest histories of either the sex of an individual dragon or of their mating rituals. We must look to the more modern Western Dragon to learn anything concrete.

Young dragons hatch from their eggs with the aid of an egg tooth.

Queen dragons are very rare. Often only one of the eggs in a laying will hatch a female. Because of this, the Western queens are well guarded by their drakes, the grouping of males in the pride. Modern fantasies extend the number of females per family but note that there is a social caste system where only a few select Queens are allowed to or capable of carrying eggs.

The social order within a dragon pride is highly structured. The dominant animal in the home territory is the breeding Queen. Within the boundaries of the caves, all dragons submit themselves to the Queen's whims and her moods. Outside the cave territory, it is the Queen's current Alpha Drake that becomes the dominant animal. During hunting and combats, the Alpha Drake leads his pack, with even the Queen acknowledging his right to rule the moment. The size, strength, and experience that comes with age is used to create a social caste system for the remaining males.

Mating occurs on the wing during a spontaneous and exhausting flight as the drakes compete to be the one strong enough or cunning enough to catch the Queen. Once the mating has occurred, the winning drake remains with the Queen until the eggs have been laid and hatched, protecting their offspring from predators. Queen dragons are anything but faithful. So with each new mating season every drake within the pride has the chance to father the clutch. It is likely that each new clutch of eggs will have a different sire, allowing for the distribution of the genes within any breeding group.

Eggs are carried within the Queen until they are well developed in size, then they are laid on either the hot sands of a sunlit beach or the sandy floor near a hot springs. The Queen guards the eggs, taking care to roll and arrange each egg for maximum heat distribution. Eggs that are laid within a cave must be warmed by the bodies of the Queen and her drake, much as birds sitting upon a nest.

After several weeks of ripening, the eggs will hatch, thanks to the added feature of an egg tooth on the fledglings. Ravenous with hunger, the little beasts must be fed quickly or they will fall upon each other in desperate hopes of finding a meal to fill their empty bellies. The wings of a newly hatched dragon are either very small or nonexistent. Some species do not grow their wing structures until late adolescence. Others are born with immature wings that will grow and strengthen with time.

The Queen dragon often laid her eggs in the warm sand, with her drake by her side.

dragons are said to have telepathic thoughts that only the most gifted humans can hear.

More mundane than their supernatural abilities are the natural defenses that dragonkind has developed through evolution. Although extremely well equipped with both claw and tooth, it is poison upon which the dragon depends the most. Venomous breath, both noxious and deadly, can melt the armor from the shoulder of a knight. Dragon skin oozes droplets of toxic sweat that can kill with just a touch. The dragon tail often sports a nasty stinger ready to stop the most determined combatant. Even the urine that is expelled during a dragon's flight is noted as causing death to any below.

One myth tells of fiery concave eyes the size of an infantryman's shield that could, by their very look, reduce the poor victim to a pile of ashes. Eyes are noted as being golden orbs that gleam red with fire, mimicking cat eyes in their depth and illusion.

With a drake, you can never be sure whether you will end up burnt by his fire breathing ability or frozen with ice from one small puff from his open mouth. The fire breathing ability of dragons is very well noted throughout history, and yet, there are no explanations given as to how the beasts accomplished this feat.

Coiling around their opponent is the favorite destructive technique of the Worms and Lindworm species. Having tightly wrapped the combatant in the center of its great bulk, the dragon begins to slowly squeeze the victim until he can no longer breathe.

Dragon Flight

It takes many years of growth for dragons to reach maturity and hone their flying skills. Because of their great body bulk, most dragons prefer to take to the air by dropping from the height of a cliff edge or a castle rampart. The beginning of the flight is then a glide that allows the wing sails to fill with air. Even with strong haunches, it takes a great deal of energy to raise a dragon's weight from a ground position. The very earth is said to groan when a dragon rises to the sky.

Once in the air, dragons soar along the air currents much like eagles or hawks, using their wings only when necessary to raise themselves into new currents. This gliding style of flight means that dragons can remain aloft for long periods of time, traveling great distances without the expenditure of large amounts of energy. The shadow of a flying dragon is said to be so large that it can block out the sun or cast an entire village into night's blackness.

Dragon Defenses

Late adolescence is the time of life in which a dragon's natural magical powers begin to be displayed. Depending on the particular legend you are following, dragons can have the power to change shapes, taking on the human form; the power to speak the language of the local populace, mesmerizing their victims with a sweet tongue; and even the power to hypnotize their victims with just a glance. Some

Castle ramparts provide an excellent starting-off point for dragons about to take flight.

Dragon Colors and Sizes

Dragons seem to come in a rainbow of colors. No color is specific to any one breed; each breed sports a range of hues and tones. The earliest dragons are said to have been golden-toned, yet red, blue, and green shades are also recorded.

The back and head skin coloring can be different from the belly tones. So a dragon that has green lizard-styled markings along its back may well have a pale yellow or gold belly section. Both the black dragon and the white dragon are very rare. The mythologies make no notation of purple dragons.

The size of a dragon can vary greatly according to its age and its species. The smallest of breeds, according to legend, are the Arabian Winged Serpents. These tiny beasts were small enough that the branches of the frankincense tree could support their body weight when the serpents wrapped their tails around the twigs to hang upside down.

At the other extreme is the dragon that was slain by Regulus, a Roman General. It took an entire legion of Roman soldiers under his command to finally destroy the 120-foot-long animal. Some dragon sizes are noted not by their length but by what they were able to eat in one meal. A dragon from Poland was said to be able to eat three oxen in one sitting.

Dragons grow in length throughout their lives. Ancient beasts can obtain tail lengths that are extremely impressive. Beards and mustaches also grow throughout a dragon's life, as do the teeth. A dragon of great age can have a tail twice the length of its belly and neck, a beard that flows down to the ground, and canine teeth that arch like massive tusks. Scales grow throughout the dragon's lifetime, reaching sizes large enough to become a soldier's shield.

Dragon Treasures

The dragon loves to collect bright, shiny objects, glimmering treasures that it personally has little use for, except to decorate his den or adorn his body. The hoarding of gold, jewelry and fine gemstones is very well documented.

Dragons collect these items while hunting and upon returning to their caves create a bed of treasures upon which they lie. Because many mythologies show that these hoards are easily found by passing humans, it must be assumed that dragons are either incapable of hiding them well or are not trying to hide these piles of gems at all. There is clear evidence to the high intelligence of the dragon species, so it is more likely that the hoards are created in such a way as to be revealed from the dragons' dens.

It may be that when dragons were solitary beasts, the drake would create a bed of gold that could be seen by a flying Queen. The Queen, in her natural attraction to bright and shiny objects, would of course stop to investigate. Thus the drake could court and woo the Queen. The larger the pile of precious gems the male dragon could create, the more likely he was to attract a Queen.

Stealing from any dragon's hoard is pure folly, as many not-so-honest men of legend have discovered. The drakes

Dragons hoard shiny objects and precious gemstones

know exactly how many and what type of objects they have collected. If these masses of wealth are indeed proportional to the drake's ability to attract a Queen, one can easily understand the dragon's ability to account for its collection.

As a final notation to the practice of hoarding, dragons also seemed to collect virgins. Beautiful human maidens appear in many legends as content captives of dragons. Once so captured, the fortunate maidens could look forward to a life of luxury and pampering by the dragons, all in exchange for a little musical entertainment, some enticing story telling, and some gentile companionship.

Dragon Mortality

In all of the ancient mythologies, all of the old legends, I have not yet found an ending to a dragon's tale that states, "and he died peacefully in his sleep at the ripe old age of — -". The records only show that the dragon is severely hunted by his sole predator and primary opponent, mankind, and therefore destined to a tragic and violent death. The means of a dragon's demise are both numerous and ingenious in their schemes.

1 Dragons that have hard scale coverings on their bodies seem impervious to the blade or the spear. However, if the knight is able to get to a position below the belly region, he will be able to slide the sword between the scales, piercing the dragon's heart.

2 Dragons that keep hoards of jewelry and gem stones will use these precious items to cover their tender underbellies, creating a waistcoat for protection. In this case, it will take an arrow or a sword blade struck deeply into the open mouth to bring the monster down.

3 If it is a Hydra that your hero faces, he will need not only a strong blade but also a flaming brand. The Hydra regrows severed heads, so the hero must cauterize the stump to prevent the dragon's natural healing process from taking place. All of the heads must be removed in this fashion. The immortal head must be buried under a large stone.

4 Only one source gives any idea to how to kill the Sea Serpent and that is A. C. Oudemans *The Great Sea-Serpent*. In it, he suggests that a harpoon laden with nitro-glycerin might do the job. However, he does warn that the weight of the exploded carcass could pull under the sailing ship that was tied to the harpoon.

5 Devoutly religious individuals seem to be lethal to the dragon. These heroes cut the beast into small pieces, then throw those pieces into a nearby sea or river. By separating each body part under the currents, the dragon is unable to reunite and heal. Dragon parts may also be buried at a crossroad. Here the dragon becomes so confused as to what direction each piece lies that it is unable to reunite.

6 One ingenious knight destined for a battle with a Worm anchored sharp blades to the outside of his armor. Then when the Worm, as Worms are prone to do, wrapped itself around the knight to squeeze him to death, the Worm was fatally sliced into tiny bits.

7 Some dragons are said to keep their hearts in a small treasure chest to protect them. Locating the box and destroying the heart will destroy the dragon. However, the knight must take care to note the dragon's location before destroying the heart. If, by chance, the dragon is flying over a village at the moment of its death, the body will fall upon the village, wiping out the very people the knight was sent to save.

8 A small village that was being devastated by a hungry dragon decided to put an end to the situation by trying to dupe the dragon. The villagers killed and skinned a large ram, stuffed the skin full of poisons and toxic substances, then sewed it back together. This decoy was left in the pasture beside the village. The passing dragon ate the ram and promptly died.

9 In Rome, it was said that a legion of skilled fighting men were sent to confront a beast that was 120 feet long. After several days of intense combat, the animal finally succumbed from the tremendous loss of blood.

10 Flaming arrows to the wings often cause the dragon's death. Also in the realm of fire fatalities are spears that have been coated with pitch, set ablaze, and thrust into the dragon's eye.

As a small addendum to this section: It is noted that even though the hero may kill the dragon, in history it was not a foregone conclusion that the knight's story would now end, "and he lived happily ever after." Many mythologies make a strong point that the hero often died as a result of battling the dragon. Stung with poisonous tail, injured by venomous bites, burnt by fire breath, or just plain exhausted, in many legends the hero and whatever familiars joined him in combat succumb at the end of the story.

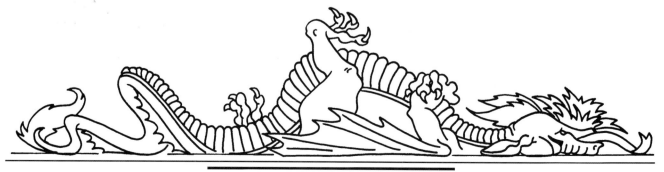

General Description of the Breeds

OR Who's who in the dragon world?

3

The many species of dragons can be sorted into groupings according to both their development physically and their roles within the legends and mythologies. Our earliest tales speak of an animal that is not much more than an oversized snake with little or no intelligence. Through the years these creatures evolve to include legs, arms, and wings, becoming more and more ornate in their adornments. Time also allows dragons to grow into cunning and skilled beasts, able foes to the heroes of our tales.

To understand which dragon is appropriate to your story, let's explore the various species and their appropriate placement in the legends.

Worm

The Worm, also spelled Worme, seems to be the oldest species of dragon recorded. It appears in legends as a legless, wingless creature that resembles a giant serpent. The Worm is noted as living in thickly forested areas near a water source such as a pond, a lake, or a swamp. It may also make its home in British hill mounds or in deep holes in the ground. Over a lifetime, the Worm can obtain tremendous size.

Much like a snake, this dragon will have smooth or finely scaled skin. The underbelly may be ridged. Several Worms of historical note have large poisonous stingers at the end of their tails as well as at the tip of their tongues. The head of this animal is shaped much

The Worm is the first of the dragons to appear in ancient legends, often being called a Giant Serpent.

like the snake with wide-set eyes and a flattened skull structure.

The Worm has an insatiable appetite, eating whatever and whomever it sees. This feeding frenzy seems to be its sole purpose of existence, and the Worm fulfills this task with great violence to the helpless victim. A solitary animal, the Worm is the dominate species of its environment. The Worm is prevalent in the "can-man-survive-against-nature" stories. Unintelligent and undirected, the Worm seems to have no control over the most base of instincts. He only exists to feed his empty belly and does so at the expense of any that come within his territory. In the shadow of his gluttony, all creatures are defenseless. As man struggles to find a small foothold of life in this huge, untamed world, the Worm becomes nature itself, the uncontrollable force that could, at any moment, erase mankind from the landscape.

And so, the Worm is used in tales of the primordial struggle by man as he tries to survive this world. It represents the unlimited, uncontrollable, and undirected power of nature.

Sea Serpent

Sea Serpents seem to fill any large body of water throughout the world. Because only the head and small arched sections of the back are visible above the water's surface, little is known about the body structure of the Sea Serpent.

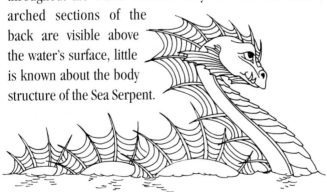

Little is known about the elusive Sea Serpent. It is reasonable to assume that a fish-scale pattern, creating a snake or eel skin effect, could adorn the body.

In the early stories the Sea Serpent is not much more than a Worm that inhabits the water instead of the land. Through time, however, the Sea Serpent has evolved to include flippers and tentacles that can reach out and pull down entire sailing ships with its weight. This dragon is often portrayed as an aquatic dinosaur.

The Sea Serpent came to represent man's fears of the unknown. As brave sailors ventured out into uncharted waters, their fears of these voyages became personified in the Serpents said to lurk at the edges of the seas. Terrible tales were told of monsters that could sink a ship with just one swat of their gigantic tailfins and of men being pulled beneath the cold waves to become the feast of the beasts. Each parting ship left port with the unspoken thoughts that should it never return the ship's demise would be due to an encounter with the great Serpent that waited for them all.

And so, as man ventured farther and farther from the small niche of safety he had established for himself within the world, the Sea Serpent became man's fear of the unknown challenges that nature held.

The Lindworm's massive body was supported by two strong forearms equipped with eagle claws.

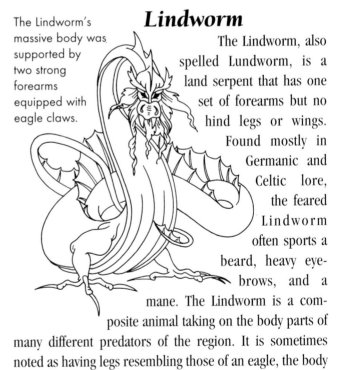

Lindworm

The Lindworm, also spelled Lundworm, is a land serpent that has one set of forearms but no hind legs or wings. Found mostly in Germanic and Celtic lore, the feared Lindworm often sports a beard, heavy eyebrows, and a mane. The Lindworm is a composite animal taking on the body parts of many different predators of the region. It is sometimes noted as having legs resembling those of an eagle, the body of a snake, and the head of a lion.

Because of the variety of animals that mythology puts together to create this new species, the Lindworm can have a wide range of looks and textures. Feather-covered legs and backs, hairy lion manes, sharp eagle claws… This creature is very open to the imagination of the artist.

Unlike its earlier cousins, the Lindworm seems to have developed some sense of reasoning and intelligence. This beast stalks mankind, seeking out his villages for food and shelter. The legends begin to include tales of hidden hoards of treasure stolen from man and guarded now by the beast. Just as mankind has grown and developed through the ages so has his greatest enemy, the dragon. The dragon is on the move. Slowly ranging outward from the deep forests and dark lakes, this beast now establishes its domain close to man's villages.

And so, the Lindworm comes to represent man's feelings that nature is purposely trying to destroy him. The Lindworm is nature as an intelligent opponent to man's survival.

Drake

The next stage of evolution in dragons is the Drake. This monster comes equipped with both front and hind legs. It appears throughout British and European art as emblems in heraldry and armaments.

The drake comes in two varieties, the fire-breathing Drake and the cold-breathing Drake. Fire Drakes are able to reduce entire villages to ashes with one puff. In reverse, the Ice Drake or Cold Drake will freeze its enemies with its breath.

Another common drake is the Oriental Dragon. This extremely long-bodied creature is noted as being responsible for causing earthquakes and tsunamis. The Drake breed is often assigned the physical attribute that fits the

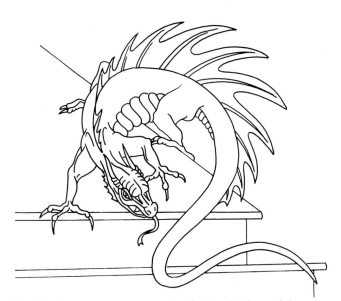

The Drake comes in two varieties: the Fire Drake and the Ice Drake.

local weather or geological conditions.

These Drakes are seen within mythology as the forces of nature in action. Fire and ice, being two basic elements within the natural world, are the two extremes wherein mankind cannot exist. The very lightning from the violent storms that can easily destroy man becomes the power of one of these twin demons. Cold so great that the victim is instantly turned to ice is the attribute of the opposite twin.

The Drake is the first of the hunting dragons, working methodically through man's herds of oxen and sheep, selectively devouring the very best of the breed. Insatiable, this monster can bring devastation to a small village's agricultural existence. Whereas in the previous mythologies the hero has had to search out the dragon hidden deep within its lair, the Drake now is the one seeking the confrontation.

And so, the Drake appears in stories as man becomes more aware of the way nature displays its powers. Whereas the Lindworm had come to take notice of mankind, the Drake has now chosen specific attributes of nature and purposefully puts them to use toward the destruction of mankind.

Hydra

Dragons come with one head only, except for the Hydra, which has multiple heads radiating from the shoulder area of the body. The number of heads changes according to the particular myth, from a

The Hydra was a multi-headed beast that appears in the Herculean tales.

British Isle Hydra with only two heads to a Hydra from the Greek legends that was said to have 100.

One of the heads on a Hydra is immortal and can not be destroyed by the blade; the other heads are mortal but will grow back if severed. Little is noted historically on the appearance of the Hydra because all the attention within the stories is focused on the terrible challenge that the multiple heads create.

This beast appears in the Herculean tales and is a monster that has seldom been repeated. It is implied through the legend that man has become painfully aware that nature has many vehicles for his destruction. Man now knows that he must be on guard at all times, for the next attack can come unexpectedly. As he battles one force of nature, the next lurks behind it, ready to strike.

This legend is of special note as the hero, Hercules, is part man part God and must be of this breeding to conquer the beast, as no mortal man would have been able to meet the challenges of the Hydra and survive. Even Hercules is placed in peril during the battle and must call upon his faithful servant for assistance. For the first time in the historical tales, the Gods and the agents of the Gods have joined man in his combat with the dragon.

And so, it is clear by the one head of the Hydra said to be immortal, that at this point in history man understands nature will outlast his breed. Therefore, no matter how well man fights his battle for survival against nature, nature will always survive him.

Winged Worm

The Winged Worm, with its huge bat-like wings, is the first of dragonkind to take to the sky.

This particular species of dragon has fully developed wings, yet no arms or legs. It is a winged snake. The wings of this worm are usually reported as being covered by a thin skin membrane, however, one winged serpent that appears in Mexican legend has full feathered bird wings and a feather-covered head and neck. Many tales tell of wonderful crests and glowing orbs for eyes.

The Winged Worm appears in mythology as the servant of the Gods, pulling great fiery chariots across the heavens.

As the histories of the Western world progress so do the enemies within its legends. The dragon's evolution to flight was inevitable, as many early creation stories tell of giant serpents that filled the heavens and of Gods that rode dragon-drawn chariots. Now, through a series of terrible battles told in the myths between the Gods and the dragon, the Gods have triumphed. The Winged Worms have become the dominion of the Gods, ready to comply to the deities' demands.

Man has turned his thoughts from nature as an uncontrolled force to place these attributes and powers within the realms of the Gods who now seem to control man's destiny. The Gods, being the personifications of man's hopes and fears, now use dragons as beasts of burden, tools, and weapons. The dragon is still nature, but now nature is under the spell cast by fickle deities.

With its submission to the Gods, the dragon has developed the ability to fly. Just as the Gods influences can be felt throughout the lives of mankind, their minions must be able to effect their wishes and whims throughout the world. By taking to wing, the dragon leaves behind the boundaries of earth and now has the heavens as its realm. The Winged Worm can appear at any time, wreaking havoc for its masters, and disappear, leaving man powerless and victimized. The dragon is no longer bound to one place or region, nor must it wait hidden within its den.

And so, the Winged Worm is the familiar to the Gods and used as their tool to wrought evil upon the innocent humans. Nature itself is now the slave of the whims and wrath of the Gods, changeable at any moment to fulfill the passions and desires of these deities.

Wyvern

The Wyvern is the first of the modern dragons, equipped with both wings and forearms. The hand at the end of the forearm is well developed and capable of grasping objects. This dragon is a common image in art and often used in the heraldry of the British Isles.

A fully established pattern of scales has appeared along with the Wyvern, and the wings have become the main ornamentation of the beast. Although more developed in the front quarters of the animal than his predecessors, this dragon still retains its serpent-like form throughout its length. The belly or underside of the Wyvern is deeply ridged or fluted to compensate for the flexibility of his

The Wyvern is the first of the modern-styled dragon. It has both wings and forelegs.

back. Pronounced canine teeth are often present as are ornate ridges along the muzzle, lower eye, and bottom jaw.

Whereas the Winged Worm came into existence during man's time of belief that there were many Gods, each with his own unique attributes both positive and negative, the Wyvern appears when man's spiritual beliefs have come to recognize only one all-powerful being. Yet, even this God is not alone, for his counterpart within the legends is the Devil, a villain as evil as this sole God is righteous.

Within the Christian legends, the Wyvern is one of the first of the beasts that will be battled over and over again by those who will become the Saints of the Church. Said to be the Devil himself, the Wyvern brought all his evils against the innocent. He spoke the language of the people, swaying their beliefs with his sweet, but forked, tongue. The Wyvern and his later cousin, the Western Dragon, are shape changers, able to deceive the eye as to their appearance. Taking on the form of a beautiful human, the Wyvern uses his cunning to manipulate the unsuspecting into wickedness.

And so, the Wyvern in these legends has evolved into an enemy to this one God that is powerful enough to be worthy of a singular foe. It is this foe, the Devil incarnate, that the dragon now represents, with the powers of Satan to lead mankind into condemnation through man's natural primal instincts. This beast appears in "man-against-the-Devil's-temptations-through-nature" stories.

Dragon or Western Dragon

The Western Dragon has it all: fully developed flight wings able to take the dragon long distances, forearms with grasping hands, and hind legs of massive strength. Its body is usually noted as being covered with heavy scales that protect tender, vital parts. This dragon has a quadruped stance yet is quite able to rear on its hind legs, leaving its hands free for combat.

The first of the Western dragons appear with a body structure common to a lizard or crocodile. The angle between the body and the leg is wide, giving the creature a low-slung profile. Over time, it begins to adopt a more mammal-like angle to the legs, allowing it to be more flexible in its movements.

The Dragon of these times is a hoarder of gold and treasure, a ravisher of domestic beasts, and a stealer of virgins. He takes anything he wants, leaving behind a terrible trail of destruction. The Western Dragon bows to no one and only the most pure and chaste can dare approach.

To the pure terror of mankind, this monster has developed supernatural powers. He not only breathes fire and ice, he is capable of mesmerizing a passing victim with a glance of his gleaming eyes. A shape changer with the full use of language, no one dares be within his presence for fear of being consumed

Fully equipped, this beast is both cunning and intelligent, a formidable foe to our heroes.

by his evil ways. Yet no one knows for sure when a dragon is present, for it may well be disguised as your beautiful wife or handsome overlord. To placate this monster, history shows mankind has offered him wealth untold to satisfy his greed, our greatest beasts to fill his belly, and our very children to relieve his lonely, vile heart.

To vanquish this demon, mankind must rise above his own nature, becoming as a God in purity and courage. The hero must combat the very evils within himself that are represented by the dragon to be purified enough to challenge the beast. Yet, even when these few souls are capable of reaching these moral heights, they are often destined themselves to die with the dragon. The Western Dragon requires an opponent that has the ability to overcome his own evil nature, but in so doing the hero is no longer human. Unwittingly and tragically, the hero has destroyed part of his humanity and therefore parishes in the end.

And so, the Western Dragon appears in legends where man must combat his own weaknesses and petty evils. We began our stories with the Worm, in which the dragon represented the uncontrollable forces of nature. With the Western Dragon we come to the point in the circle of stories where man now versus the nature within himself in an attempt to rise above his own passions and ultimately conquer nature.

Fairy Dragon

Many species seem to have at least one miniature breed, and dragons are no exception. No bigger than a dragonfly, the Fairy Dragon is said to have translucent insect wings. Fairy dragons have all the attributes of their larger cousins and are noted for their mischievous behavior. These delightful little beasts are the familiars of elves and fairies, often

This mischievous creature is likely to guide you down the wrong path or hide your trinkets.

living within their homes as favored pets. They are also found in mushroom clusters and in small, floral-covered thickets near the forest's edge.

Because Fairy Dragons are not very big at all, they no longer have the evil impact on man's life that their larger cousins once had. Instead they are most likely to be mere nuisances, playing mischievous pranks on the unsuspecting. Untying boot laces, hiding small trinkets, and guiding a traveler along the wrong fork in the road are favorite games of this tiny species.

Fantasy Dragon

The Fantasy Dragon, the newest species of the breed, also appears in contemporary literature as familiars and friends. The scales of the Fantasy Dragon are less pronounced and they may have a soft leather-like appearance. Large gentle eyes portray their compassion and wisdom.

These beasts are man's constant companions and life-long mates. Bonding at hatching through a form of telepathy with specially endowed humans, these beasts spend their years serving mankind in his struggle to survive. They are noted as being loving, loyal, and dedicated to their human partners, willing to risk their lives for the protection of these blessed individuals. Looking much like their Western Dragon cousins, the Fantasy Dragon no longer is an evil counterpart to man, but now represents all the goodness within the human race.

And so, our tales began with mankind in a constant struggle for survival against the forces of nature, the dragon. Yet having battled his own evil nature and having discovered a godlike part to himself when confronting the Western Dragon, man is now at peace with nature, both in the world that surrounds him and within himself. The Dragon can now develop into the personification of goodness. The beast has been allowed its own place within man's world just as man has found his place within nature. Man, no longer needing to fight nature, can now embrace it, making dragonkind man's friend.

The circle of legends is now complete. Man has discovered through his journeys in the legends and myths that he is nature, and therefore is the dragon.

Basic Anatomy

OR What's inside the dragon that lets it move?

4

The dragon, of course, is an unknown creature, a composite of many commonly known animals pulled into one new beast. As artists, we may find this poses an interesting problem: We have no exact structure from which to work. Each dragon seems to be unique, taking on whatever body structures and appearances are appropriate to the story and the time period.

Artists are well cautioned to remember that viewers of the artwork bring their knowledge of the real world into the realm of the mythology and use that knowledge to judge the art. As an example, the viewer knows that the crocodile's body lies close to the ground and that it is unable to raise its head more than a few inches. The walking movement comes not from the swing of the legs but from the shifting of the shoulder joints, giving the croc the appearance of twisting as it moves.

So, if as artists, we design a dragon obviously modeled from the crocodile, yet show the creature with its head raised high, arched over its back, walking smoothly through the scene, the viewer will be troubled. From the viewer's base of knowledge, this position would not be possible and therefore not believable.

First determining what attributes your dragon is to have and how those attributes appear in nature will help you to define your animal as a believable creation.

MAMMAL OR A REPTILE

Dragons come in two different body styles: the mammal-bodied worm and the reptile-bodied worm. Each body style has its own unique set of joints. The way that the shoulder and hip joints are formed determines several characteristics of the dragon, including the way its body lies to the ground, the height that it can raise its head, and the footprint pattern that will be left by its passing. In general, mammals have joints that allow the limbs of the animal to lie parallel to the body, whereas the joints of a reptile's body hold the limbs perpendicular to the body.

Mammal-Styled Bodies

The body of a mammalian dragon is supple and limber, easily twisted into tight knots and curls. (See Figure 1a.) The strong spinal muscles allow the dragon to use the lower belly area as an anchor and raise its head high above the surrounding landscape. The head is well jointed at the top of a long, tapering neck. The jointed spine allows the dragon to use one of its strongest hunting strategies, that of curling itself around the hapless victim and squeezing it to death.

Wing joints are located at the base of the neck where the neck flows into the top of the chest barrel. (See Figure 1b.) This joint allows for a full swing; the dragon can bring its wings up well above its head or lay them flat along its back.

When at rest in a sitting position, the wings will be arched above the joint. Only when the dragon is angry or sleeping will the wings be pulled tightly to the body along the back. In a folded position, the wings will lie along the back of the dragon, overlapping as birds' wings. Similar to a bird at rest, little or none of the dragon's back is visible when the wings are in a reclined posture, tucked up against the body.

The foreleg's shoulder joint shares the area where the wing joint attaches to the body. (See Figure 1c.) Dragons, unlike any animal in nature, can have up to three sets of limbs, one set of wings and one set each of forelegs and hind legs. Looking to the natural world, we find that the wing structures of birds or bats are forelegs that have developed into appendages that can support flight. So, in essence, the dragon has two sets of forelegs: one that has developed into wings and one that remains as legs with grasping hands. As a result, the wing's shoulder joint and the foreleg's shoulder joint fall into the same general area on the torso, most likely sharing the ball cup joint located in the shoulder blade. The wings are placed above the foreleg joint in this example. They may also be placed in the aft position, depending on the posture of your dragon.

Forelegs, or arms, are fully articulated, ending in clawed hands that are able to grasp small, fine objects. The forelegs at rest lie against the body with the upper part of the foreleg coming into contact with the belly.

The hind legs are also fully articulated, lying at a point at the end of the belly area. (See Figure 1d.) As with the forelegs, the hind legs are placed parallel to the body of the animal. The elbows of the forearm are opposed to the

Figure 1a: Mammal Body Style
The spine of a mammal-bodied dragon is extremely flexible, allowing the animal to curl and twist easily.

Figure 1b: Mammal Wing Position
The wing is a foreleg that has developed the structures necessary for flight. It lies at the top of the chest barrel where the neck joins the body.

Figure 1c: Mammal Forelegs
Forelegs share the joint area with the wings. Because wings are specialized forearms, the dragon has, in essence, two sets of arms: one for grasping and one for flying.

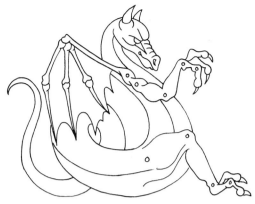

Figure 1d: Mammal Hind Legs
The hind legs are strong and powerful, able to hold the dragon in a standing position or push the dragon from the ground, launching it into flight.

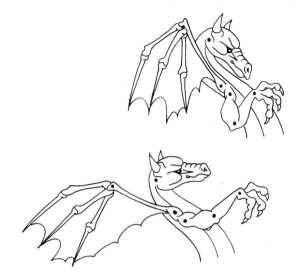

Figure 1e: Mammal Wing Movement
The mammal-styled wing structure can provide a wide range of movement and positioning. Whether fully extended or contracted, this area has at least five joints which the artist can manipulate.

knees of the hind legs, giving the dragon the gait of a horse or a dog. Again, the hind leg ends with a clawed foot capable of holding on to the surrounding support structures such as cliff edges and castle walls.

The tail is at least equal in length to the total length of the body, neck and head combined. This proportion will change according to the age of the dragon. A young dragon, called a dragonette, has a short tail that grows throughout its lifetime. By middle age, the tail of the dragon has grown to be equal to the length of its body. By old age, a dragon's tail can become extremely impressive in the length it achieves.

Dragons are able to stand fully erect on their hind legs. A few species are even depicted as walking on their hind legs. However, the most common dragon stance found in art history is that of using all four legs to walk, the stance of a quadruped. This allows the artist to position the dragon in the art along the horizontal line, resting on three legs, with the fourth leg, usually a foreleg, reaching or grasping the dragon's opponent. Experiment with other stances, keeping in mind the limits of the dragon's anatomy.

Reptile-Styled Bodies

The reptilian worm is a cold-blooded vertebrate with a low-slung body profile. The barrel of the chest is supported by short stocky legs and rides close to the ground. Unlike the mammalian version of the worm, the reptilian worm has limbs that extend away from the body at a 90-degree angle. Many of the earliest tales use crocodiles or lizards as the archetype of the breed, hence the common name, Winged Lizard, that appears in mythology.

The head is carried above the chest on a short neck. (See Figure 1f.) The neck has little flexibility, so the reptilian dragon must swing its entire upper body to change the position of its head. This dragon would be unable to bend its neck around to look over its shoulder.

The body is also very static in its mobility. A crocodile-styled dragon would be unable to coil its girth around an opponent. For this dragon, an attack or defense would need to be either from the head or from the swinging of its tail.

As with the mammalian dragon, the wings of a reptilian dragon will join the top of the chest barrel at the base of the neck. (See Figure 1g.) Because the limbs in a reptile are jointed to the body at a right angle to the spinal column, we can assume that the wings of the dragon would also have a perpendicular placement. Here the wing limbs fold against the side of the dragon's body instead of along its back.

The forelegs of the reptilian dragon, just as with those of the mammalian dragon, share the ball socket joint with the wings. (See Figure 1h.) These forelegs angle first away from the body, then bend down toward the ground. The grasping hands will also face away from the torso. Note the wide stance of the forelegs in the illustration.

The forearms will have little mobility, and the ability to walk comes through the dragon swinging its entire body at the shoulder area. Imagine for a moment the gait of a crocodile: It swings its upper body and head to create the movement for walking. So it is with a reptilian dragon.

Hind legs complete this dragon and are positioned exactly as the forelegs. (See Figure 1i.) Whereas the elbow and knee joints are opposed in a mammalian dragon, in a reptilian dragon, the elbow and knee joints point in the same direction, slightly back from the body. These legs also receive their movement from the shifting of the body at the hip area.

The final gait for a reptilian dragon has a very angular appearance. As the crocodile walks, it swings his head, shoulders and hips. Therefore, if it thrusts its front left leg forward, it will arch its back. Next, it will keep its forelegs in place while swinging its right hind leg forward. This will give it a semi-circular line through the spine, with the circle being created by the right foreleg and the right hind leg. This jointing, although it is not compatible with long distance speed, does afford the dragon great strength in lunging as a primary attack.

GENERAL SKELETAL STRUCTURES

Exploring the skeletal structure of the dragon gives

Figure 1f: Reptile Body Style
The bodies of reptilian dragons hug the ground, their heads barely rising above their legs.

Figure 1g: Reptile Wing Position
Wings lie perpendicular to the shoulder joint and will fold along the sides of the body, not the back.

Figure 1h: Reptile Forelegs
The forelegs of the reptilian dragon create a right angle to the torso then drop to the ground with a second right angle at the elbow joint.

Figure 1i: Reptile Hind Legs
The dragon will takes on a wide stance where the individual foot prints will be far apart from the center line of the torso.

the artist a chance to determine the possible positions and movements the beast can obtain. A sample skeleton can be created from parts of known species. (See Figure 2a.) The skeleton of the sample dragon comprises a crocodile-styled skull, a mammal's spine and legs, an eagle's claws, and a bird's or bat's wings. This combination allows for the dragon's known flexibility, its four-legged stance, and its capacity for flight.

The Wing and Shoulder Joint

The most unusual feature of the Western Dragon is its three sets of limbs: wings, forearms, and hind legs. (See Figure 2b.) Doing a few rough sketches of the dragon quickly shows that these are several areas that will need special attention and special solutions.

The first concern is the shoulder area along the spine. Forearms will join the spine at the shoulder joint, but so will wings, as they are simply forearms that have developed flight capacity. Now, two sets of limbs come into the spine at the same area. This dilemma could be solved by giving each set of limbs its own shoulder joint, yet this would be opposed to the natural world—no known animal has two sets of shoulder blades. It is difficult enough as an artist to compensate for three sets of limbs, but adding double shoulder blades becomes too much for the artist and ultimately the viewer.

The natural solution is to allow the wings and forearms to share the shoulder joint. In this way, the wing and fore-arm are united into one smoothly flowing line from the wing tip to the claw tip. The ball joint is placed at the top of the shoulder joint. It could have just as easily been positioned to the front or rear of the shoulder, depending on the final position of the dragon in the painting or artwork, as long as it falls into the common area along the spine.

The next area of concern is the claws at the end of the forearms and hind legs. Throughout history, these claws are referred to as being the claws of an eagle, yet the dragon tales tell us these claws were quite capable of grasping, holding, and using objects. A bird of prey can indeed grasp an object, but it does not have enough flexibility within the claw to manipulate the item. So we end up with a structure that has the appearance of a bird's claw but the mobility of a primate's hand. This would imply an opposable "claw" on the forearm that faces in toward the body when at rest and jointed so that it can move through an arc from the front of the hand back toward the wrist.

The last area to be explored is the hind leg and hip joint. Again, the dragon is in the unique position of having three sets of limbs. Where the hind legs fall along the spine has a direct impact on how well the dragon will be able to walk. If this hip joint is placed too far away from the shoulder joint, the dragon will have the appearance of an Oriental Dragon. Orientals do have the ability to walk, but the jointing positions imply that they drag a large section of their bellies along the ground as they move. In essence, Orientals slither like a snake with the added benefit of legs

Figure 2a: Because we have no actual dragon skeletons to work from, we must create a skeleton by using a composite of known animals.

Figure 2b: The dragon has three sets of limbs. The wing structure and foreleg bones share a common shoulder joint. The hind legs are positioned along the spine according to the span of the dragon's gait.

Figure 2c: Because this dragon has wings, it will also have an exaggerated wishbone and sternum to anchor the flight muscles.

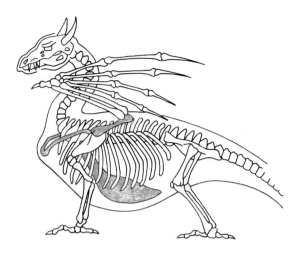

Figure 2d: As the wing position changes, so will the position of the wishbone and sternum, thus changing the profile lines along the neck and chest belly.

to help push their massive weight forward. To determine hip placement, first decide how your dragon will walk; then adjust the distance between the shoulder and hip to accommodate this gait. The more upright the dragon is the closer these two joints will lie along the spine.

Another area to consider along with hip placement is the length of the bones of the forearms and the hind legs. The farther away these limbs are from one another, the shorter the limb bones will be. The crocodile has its hind legs well away from the shoulder and thus has very short legs, allowing the body to hug the ground. As the hind leg moves forward along the spine, the legs become longer, as in a dog or a horse. The giraffe has very close-set shoulder and hip joints, allowing it the luxury of extremely long legs.

Wings

That the dragon has wings, and therefore the ability to fly, implies a great deal about the skeletal structure of the beast. Wings are forearms that have either a covering of feathers, as birds, or a covering of a strong but thin membrane, as bats. The bones that would have been hands have become elongated to support this covering. The opposable thumb points toward the head of the creature and the four fingers have become the stays of the wing membrane.

Wings also imply changes internally for our creature. As birds developed flight, every aspect of their bodies was adapted to accommodate this mobility. Bones became hollow to make them lightweight,;the carina (wishbone) and sternum (central chest bone) became exaggerated. These

two bones help to counter-balance the bird's body during flight, making it possible to change direction in flight. An extra large sternum is necessary to anchor the flight muscles through the chest area.

Note in the illustration that the carina, the sternum and the first bone in the wing are shaded. (See Figure 2c.) These three bones work together to determine the shape of the chest and the positioning of the wings. As you work on your dragon's skeleton, treat these three bones as one unit. When you move one, move them all.

If the dragon is at rest, the first bone of the wing drops down, parallel to the spine. (See Figure 2d.) This position will shift the carina so that it is also parallel to the backbone and cause the sternum to drop deeper into the chest cavity. This implies that when at rest the dragon will have a prominent ridge created by the carina where the neck and chest meet and a thickened barrel shape to the chest. How the wings lie along the dragon's back determines the profile of the neck and chest line, and the barrel width of the chest area.

When the dragon raises its wings, it pulls the carina and sternum up into to the chest cavity. (See Figure 2e.) The carina and first wing bone are now perpendicular to the spine and the sternum is hidden within the rib cage. The ridge that was at the area where the neck meets the chest has now dropped to a position between the dragon's front legs. Its chest barrel has narrowed. Note also that as the first wing bone is extended, the finger bones of the wing expand.

Figure 2c: If the wings are raised, the chest barrel will narrow and the wishbone will drop to a position between the dragon's forelegs.

Figure 2d: The more joints your dragon has, the more mobile it will be. Dragons can be twisted, folded and curled into marvelous positions within your art.

Developing wings gave the bird another unusual aspect to its skeletal structure: The number of bones in its neck are greatly increased. Land mammals, such as a horse or a dog, have seven neck bones. These bones enlarge in size as the animal does, but the number does not change. The giraffe has the same number of neck bones as the mouse; both can swing their heads only 180-degrees.

However, birds have twenty-five neck bones that allow for a swing of nearly 360 degrees, or a full circle. This expanded number of joints allows the bird to turn its head over its back. As an example, an owl sitting on a branch with its back toward you can turn its head to face you and continue turning. The dragon, because it has flight capacities, also has this neck mobility. It, too, can turn its long neck to lay its head along its backbone ridge. Keep in mind though, that this rule only applies if the dragon is equipped with wings. Worms and non-winged serpents will not have the ability to swing their heads in a full circle.

Joints

That the dragon has three sets of limbs can pose a problem for the artist, but when it comes to mobility, that extra set becomes an asset to your dragon. More limbs means more joints that can move and be positioned within the artwork. (See Figure 2f.) Make a note on your dragon's skeleton as to where each joint will be. These are places that you can bend, fold and twist to place your dragon in wonderfully flowing shapes.

Because the dragon in the example is based on a mammal's structure, it can sit down on its haunches, raise its wings, and lift one arm toward its opponent, all while holding on to its hoard of gold!

WING STRUCTURES

Dragons can have one of at least three types of wings: bat wings, bird wings or butterfly wings. Try to match the style of wings to the overall style of the dragon for the best look. For example, butterfly wings on a very large, very scaly, fire-breathing dragon would look out of place, whereas bat wings that end in claws would fit perfectly.

Bat Wings

Bat-winged dragons have strong, bony stays that run the full length of the wing from shoulder to wing tip. The joint areas of the wing stays are very prominent. Over these support structures a fine, but tough membrane of skin is drawn to create the sail. The membrane can be smooth, roughly textured, and even covered with fine hair or down feathers.

How the membrane finishes at the end of the sail is individual to each dragon. Some wings end in a smooth arch reaching from stay to stay; others might have a serrated look with a multitude of arched points between the stays.

The bat wing stays may end in a claw, because the stays are indeed a forearm that has developed flight capacity. Some grasping ability could be attributed to the wing.

Figure 3a: Bat wings have thin, but sturdy membranes stretched over the finger bones that create the stays of the wings.

Figure 3b: Eagle wings are a common structure for historic dragons. Long accent feathers can be added to the back of the head and neck.

There is often an extra claw at the top of the structure created from the stay that would have been the forearm's thumb.

Bird Wings

The same bony stay structure is found in the bird-like wings of a dragon, however, with the addition of feathering the underlying structure is not apparent. A bird-winged dragon will still have the same jointing in the wing and the ability to fold or bend the flight structure.

Feathering can become quite exaggerated, with long trailing flight feathers at the tip or bottom edge of the wing. If your dragon is to have a feathered wing, it may also have feathers covering its head, neck and upper chest. Only the length of the tail and the back would be smooth-skinned or scaled. The tail may end in a small puff of ornamental down.

Butterfly Wings

The Fairy Dragon has a set of wings unique unto its species—those of an insect. Which particular insect wings you use will depend on your conception of this tiny dynamo. Butterfly wings, dragonfly wings, and even bumble bee wings are all appropriate.

Indeed, the Fairy Dragon poses the same complex

problem to scientists as does the bumble bee. Studies and research have shown that the small wing structure of the bumble bee should not be able to support the insect's large body in flight, yet not only does this bee fly, it flies with great control and precision. So does the Fairy Dragon.

Figure 3c: Fairy Dragons have the wings of a dragonfly or butterfly.

Adding Ornamentation

5

OR How do I give a dragon a face lift?

ach dragon seems to have its own face, features and ornamentations that are unique to it and appropriate to its story. Just as we used sketches of the skeleton to explore the positioning of the beast, using a simple skull sketch will aid in creating the animal's final appearance.

THE DRAGON'S SKULL

The sample illustration is a line drawing of a crocodile-style skull. (See Figure 4a.) Note the heavy brow ridges that protect the eye socket, the central ridge line over the forehead where the powerful neck muscles attach to the skull, and the bulges along the mouth line that accommodate the enlarged cutting teeth. The lower jaw is massive at the back to anchor the jaw muscles.

Begin by taking the line drawing for the skull into a shaded or contoured pencil drawing. (See Figure 4b.) This will give you an idea of how each area flows into the next and bends throughout the entire skull. You can see how the crocodile's skull is angular, almost box-like in its construction.

As illustrated, break the skull into related planes using the natural, angular shape as your guide. (See Figure 4c.) The top of the skull, forehead, and muzzle have become distinct areas along the top of the skull, dropping off at the nostril ridge. Along the sides of the upper skull, the mouth seems to break into two areas: the first, in line with the eye socket, running from the eye to the nostrils; and the second, becoming the upper mouth, running from under the eye to a central point at the bottom of the nostril. Behind the eye socket is a large flat plate that becomes the side of the dragon's head.

The lower jaw is composed of two separate planes: one large area at the back of the jaw to hold the chewing muscles and one plane that narrows as it approaches the nostril. This second plane becomes the lower mouth.

By breaking the skull down further into groupings of planes, you will be able to see which areas of the skull are related. (See Figure 4d.) This illustration has eight units: the upper skull, the forehead, the muzzle, the nostril area, the temple, the eye socket, the upper mouth, and the lower jaw line. Ornamentation can now be added to each area to

give the dragon its unique features.

Use the general shape and direction of each plane to begin this work. Horns have been added to the upper skull and the temple region. (See Figure 4e.) Ridges have been added to the muzzle area to give a small amount of texturing along the top of the face. Heavy serrated eyebrow ridges emphasize the bony overhang of the upper eye socket. Small horns accent the upper mouth and the teeth are exaggerated. Along the lower back jaw, a new set of horns protrude in a ridged pattern.

When you have a working sketch of the individual plane groups, reunite them into one skull. (See Figure 4f.) You can easily make any necessary adjustments or additions. Be sure to check that the dragon can still close its mouth and that no ornamentation overlaps any other.

Finally, return the skull to a contoured pencil drawing,

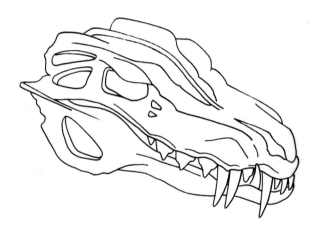

Figure 4a: Begin with a line drawing of a crocodile's skull.

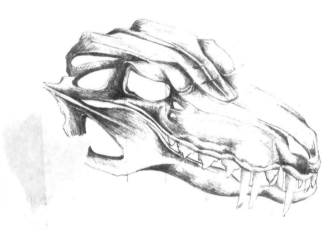

Figure 4b: Use a soft pencil to create a contour of the skull.

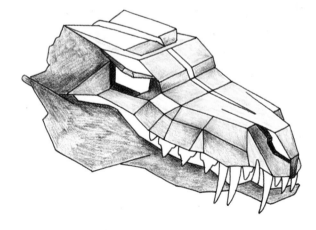

Figure 4c: Break the skull into sections of flat planes, noting each area with a colored pencil.

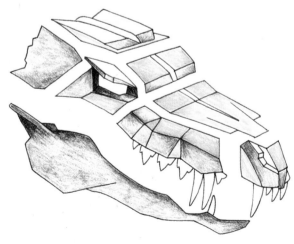

Figure 4d: Separate the planes into groupings according to the facial structure.

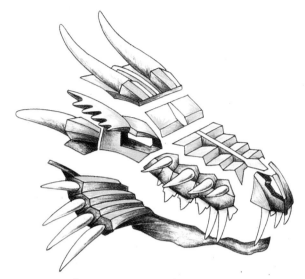

Figure 4e: Use these groupings to plan your ornamentations.

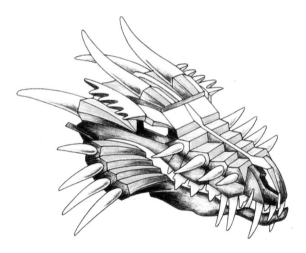

Figure 4f: Reconnect the groups of planes, putting the individual pieces back together.

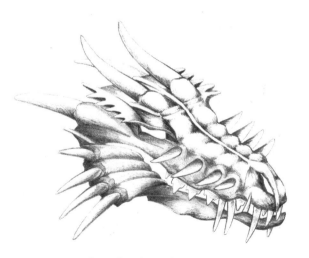

Figure 4g: Transform the planes back into a contour drawing. You are now ready to add skin and texture to this dragon's head.

smoothing out the angular look of the planes. (See Figure 4g.) This dragon is now ready to have a skin or scale covering to complete his look.

FIRE BREATHING DRAGONS

Opening the mouth on a pattern to accommodate fire breath is a fairly simple matter. Begin with a tracing of the head of the dragon. (See Figure 5a.) In nature it is the bottom jaw that moves up and down. However, in art, this poses a problem when you are working with pre-established patterns. Lowering the bottom jaw can cause the mouth to lay into the belly area of the dragon or it can direct the fire down toward the dragon's feet.

Instead of moving the lower jaw, raise the upper area of the skull and upper jaw. This will give you more control over both the neck and the head positions, as well as the direction of the breath.

Find the point in the back skull area where the horns or ears would be located. (See Figure 5b.) This point in the upper half of the back of the head is approximately halfway between the eye and the back of the skull.

Using this point and the back corner of the mouth, draw a line. (See Figure 5c.) From the skull point, draw a second line that is perpendicular to the mouth line.

With scissors cut the tracing along the mouth line and the perpendicular line that runs through the top of the skull. (See Figure 5d.) Pivoting on the point in the skull, move the upper portion of the pattern until the mouth is opened appropriately. Note that I am moving the area of the face that contains the eyes, the muzzle and the nostrils.

Retrace the pattern, smoothing out the line along the top of the skull. (See Figure 5e.) The back corner of the mouth now becomes a box shape where the cheek connects the upper and lower jaws.

The breath comes from deep within the throat, not from the front of the mouth. (See Figure 5f.) It can be either a tongue of flame as shown here or a cloud effect where everything around the mouth and muzzle is alight.

Figure 5a: Trace the basic head shape of the dragon, leaving out any ornamentation.

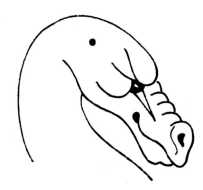

Figure 5b: Mark the point where the ears or horns would be located.

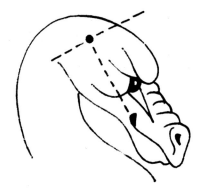

Figure 5c: Draw a line from the corner of the mouth to the point you marked in the previous step and a second line perpendicular to the first line.

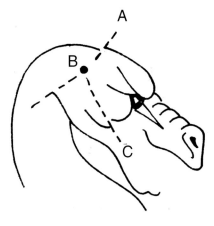

Figure 5d: Cut the pattern apart from point A to point B and from point B to point C. Reposition the pattern using B as a pivot point.

Figure 5e: Redraw the lines of the head, smoothing out the areas you changed.

Figure 5f: Add ornamentation. Make sure that the facial accents will not become entangled in the fire breath.

Figure 5g: Add fire in a flame (as shown here) or as a cloud.

CHOOSING ORNAMENTATIONS

Once you understand the make-up of the skull, adding ornamentation that is both believable and attractive is easy. There is a huge variety of possibilities from which you can choose to decorate your individual dragon.

This section begins with a simple dragon's head (above). This dragon has an obvious forehead stop that leads into a ridged muzzle. The nostril area is prominent. Note the line along the lower jaw that leads into the neck.

Horns

Along the upper skull we can add horns. These are placed above the eye line and centrally located between the eye and the back of the skull. Some dragons will have only one horn, however multiple horns decorating the top or side of the skull are not uncommon.

Horn Ideas
- Horns that arch toward the face
- Horns that arch away from the face toward the neck
- Multiple horns placed down the central ridge of the skull
- Horns that curl in a full circle, similar to those of a ram
- A unicorn horn at the center of the forehead

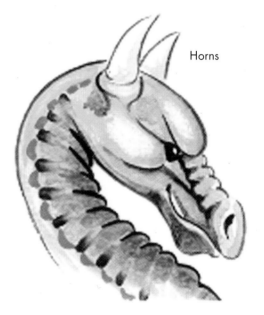

Horns

Ears

Below the horn is the placement for the ears. Again centrally located in the back region of the skull the top of the ear lies along the line from the eye to the back of the head.

Ear Ideas
- Elf-like ears that come to a sharp point
- Horse or mule-like ears that are folded and rounded at the tips
- Cow-like ears that project away from the face
- Tufted ears like an owl's

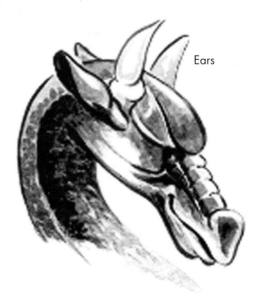

Ears

Crests

Crests

Historically, crests are the most common ornament sported by dragons. The type of crest varies dramatically from legend to legend. Beginning at the edge of the forehead, the crest can end at the base of the skull or flow down into the neck line.

Crest ideas
- Fish-like fins with heavy spines
- Serrated or paneled crests, like a dinosaur
- Thick manes of hair
- Masses of tentacles

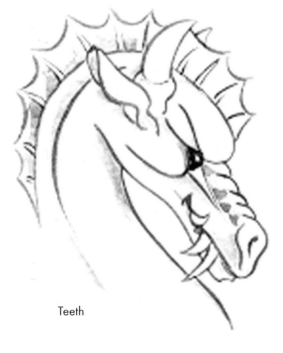

Teeth

Teeth

Of course, a dragon needs teeth. Teeth can protrude from the upper jaw or the lower jaw.

Teeth Ideas
- Upper arching canine teeth
- Downward arching cutting teeth
- Boar's tusks
- Fine needle-like teeth

Small Crests

Small crests along the back jaw line can give a lizard-like feeling to the face. Start the crest on the jaw just below the end of the mouth. Add one small crest along the center line of the jaw so that it flows down into the neck. The dragon will display this ornament well when his head is raised. Two small crests can be used, one on each side of the lower jaw. The crest can also make a ring or loop around the face, beginning at one end of the jaw, looping around the front of the chin then ending on the other side of the jaw.

Small Crest Ideas
- Serrated fins with spine supports
- Fish like side fins
- Loosely fold skin flaps

Small Crests

Beards

Beards seem to be a common decoration for dragons especially when the beast has lived many years. The dragon's beard grows from the lower jaw with the teeth overlapping the hair. Hair is not the only chin ornament. This area can also be accented with tentacles, horns, or spikes.

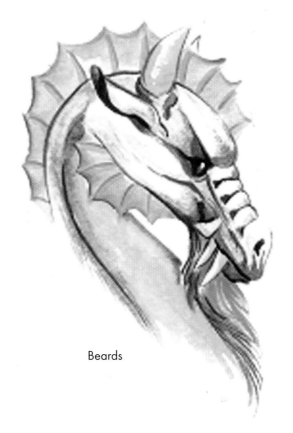

Beards

Mustaches

Mustaches adorn the upper lip of the jaw radiating from the sides of the nostril ridge. Just as with the beard these can be hair, tentacles, fine horns, or spikes.

Fluting

The neck is a rich area for adding details, fluting or scales along the belly section can flow into deeply knobbed crocodile skin. Let the belly area of the neck begin just behind the ears of the dragon.

Fire

An open mouth can be filled with a long, slithering tongue, fire breath, or ice breath, depending on the dragon's characteristics. Note how the beard, mustache and fire all flow away from the dragon. (See the preceding section, page 34, for specific information on correctly opening the dragon's mouth.)

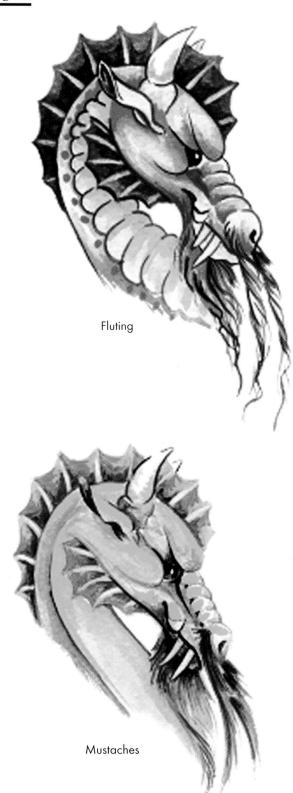

Fluting

Fire

Mustaches

Scale
Work

6

OR How do I keep a dragon from looking like a fish?

There are several alternatives to skin texture that you can use on your dragon. Scaling, creating a meshwork of fine rounded curves that overlap and flow from head to tail, is the most common. Historically, however, dragons also come in feathers, reptile skin, smooth eel-like skin, and even colored patterns.

SCALING

How you place the scales within the grid work is unlimited. Parallel rows, staggered rows, rounded scales, pointed scales, even hairy scales can be created. In the sample of scaling patterns, you will find some simple ideas that may help you to create your own textures.

Scales can be set in parallel rows giving a ridged effect from head to tail, or they can be offset one row to the next, working from the center points of the two scales above. Again, you can use rounded scales, arrow heads, convex scales…. Any basic shape can be transformed into a dragon's scales. Mix and match scale patterns using small units along the belly edge and larger units down the center of the spine.

Change both the shape and size of the scales as they travel across the dragon's form. Small scales can be used around the face, jaw line, and upper neck. As the body diameter of the dragon increases so will the size of the scaling. Also consider changing the coloring of the scales from area to area. Fine texturing along the belly ridge and face may be darker than the large scales along the back.

The scales down the spine on this sample are very large, plate-like units. (See Figure 6a.) To each side of these central plates lay two rows of small, rounded scaling. The belly is simple ribbing with a fine line between each section. This layout, using a larger scale for the center of the back, is excellent for any dragon that shows more of its spine than its belly.

Inside each of the large scales add a small spiked area for color. This pointed accent picks up the stays in the chin fin and the horns along the crest of the skull. The rows are laid out parallel to give a long slender look to the neck.

In this sample, the scale shapes are varied from unit to unit, round to arrowhead. (See Figure 6b.) You do not have to keep the scale pattern the same throughout the body of the animal. By changing patterns you can add interest to the scale work. Again the layout is in parallel rows, however by changing the units within those rows your eye moves back and forth from scale to scale. Here, we end up with a diagonal finish to the skin.

Because this dragon has some serration to the chin fin and the head mane, the addition of the arrowhead scales keeps the pattern of points throughout the dragon.

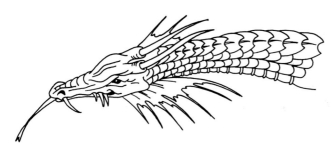

Figure 6a: Large scales down the center of the spine emphasizes the back.

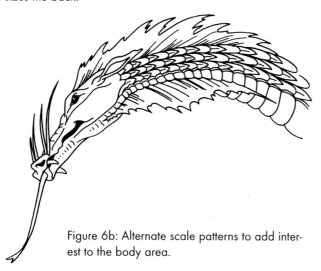

Figure 6b: Alternate scale patterns to add interest to the body area.

Reptile Skin

Hobnailing, in which the skin is broken into bubble-like sections along the back and upper sections of the legs, is a common texture for reptiles. (See Figure 6c.) Because we must assume some kinship of the dragon to common reptiles, we can carry the idea of hobnailing into the skin textures available to us as artists. For this sample, the texturing flows from the sides of the neck into the cheeks of the face. To create a visual demarcation between the back and belly, the belly ribbing has been sectioned into very thin slices.

This style of skin texturing is created with the use of shadowing between each hobnailed section and brighter highlights on the top edges of the bubbles.

Feathers

The scale work on this dragon is very minimal; there is only a small amount under the jaw line as the head leads into the neck. (See Figure 6d.) These very fine scallops accent the feather work along the upper neck. Many early dragons were said to have the head and claws of an eagle, therefore implying that feathers are an acceptable body covering.

This would be an appropriate animal in which to carry the feathering through on the wings and tail tip. The main areas of the body, those not covered with feathers would be smooth skin.

Colored Patterns

Often the dragon is compared to the snake and so offers us a range of colored patterns that we can used to decorate the beast. Snakes do have extremely fine scaling, but it is the arrangement of the colors in bands, diamonds, and stripes that give them their unique appearance. This sample dragon has large scaled belly ribs, but his neck and back are decorated through a changing color design. Note that the pattern is carried through to the face, beneath the eyes, and along the muzzle ridge.

Figure 6c: Hob-nailed skin texture, similar to that of reptiles, can be used.

Figure 6d: Not all dragons have reptile or fish-styled scales; some come with feathers.

Figure 6e: Colorful snake-skin patterns can be created as your final texturing.

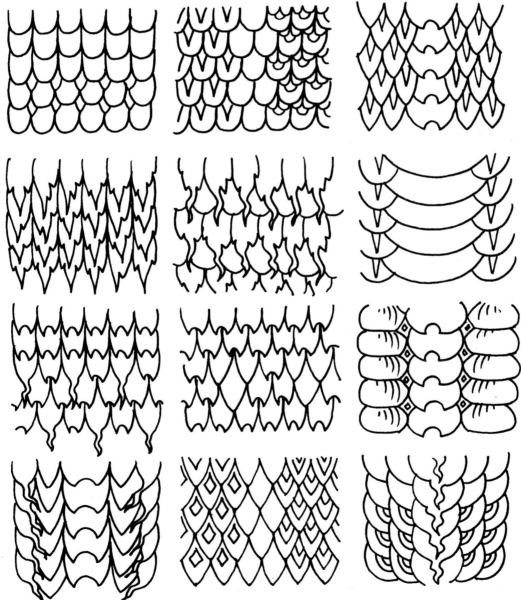

Scales can be laid out in many different patterns. By creatively changing the shape, size and texture, each dragon can become unique.

SCALE GRID WORK

Scales and plating are created along a basic grid work that flows throughout the entire beast. (See Figure 7a.) This grid pattern will need to be added to many of the designs in this book. How large you make each unit within the grid will determine how large each scale will be. Plus, the size of the scales will change as the diameter of the dragon's body changes. By changing these factors, you can create hundreds of different dragons from the patterns in this book.

Note first on your design which area is body and which is belly. You may wish to work each area individually to allow for different scaling, plating, or ridge lines.

Begin with the horizontal lines throughout the dragon's body. (See Figure 7b.) Follow the folded body area on

Figure 7a: Working with guide lines will make the addition of scaling, plating, and ribbing much easier.

Figure 7b: The guide lines can be put into place by eye. Begin with the horizontal lines that run from the top of the head to the tip of the tail.

Figure 7c: Vertical grid lines are added next. Many units will become pie-shaped to allow for the changing shape of body's curves.

Figure 7d: Continue adding grid lines until you have enough units to accommodate the size and layout of your scaling.

our sample dragon, just behind the tip of the tail as a guide. Visually note the location of the middle of this area, then make a pencil mark. Next, visually divide each side of the body from this mark into three units. Make a mark for each.

Continue these marks, shown as dashes, throughout the dragon's body. Connect the dashes, creating horizontal lines. As you work you will see that the lines narrow as the body of the dragon narrows. In some areas you will wish to begin reducing the number of verticals as that area reduces in size. Note how the lines change at the end of the tail and at the neck where it comes off the chest.

Work the vertical lines in the same manner. (See Figure 7c.) Begin by dividing the dragon's body at the center, divide each remaining area in half, then divide each of these areas into half units.

Just as with the horizontal guides, the vertical guides will vary in width. Note the main curl in the body just behind the tail tip. The length of the body along the inside curve is much smaller than the length of the body along the outside curve. Therefore your units will become pie-shaped, allowing each unit to compensate for the changes created by the curling.

Continue working each set of guidelines until your have a grid work created that is appropriate to the size of the scaling you will be using. (See Figure 7d.) Scales, plates, and ribs can now be penciled onto your dragon so that they follow both the curve and flow of the dragon's body.

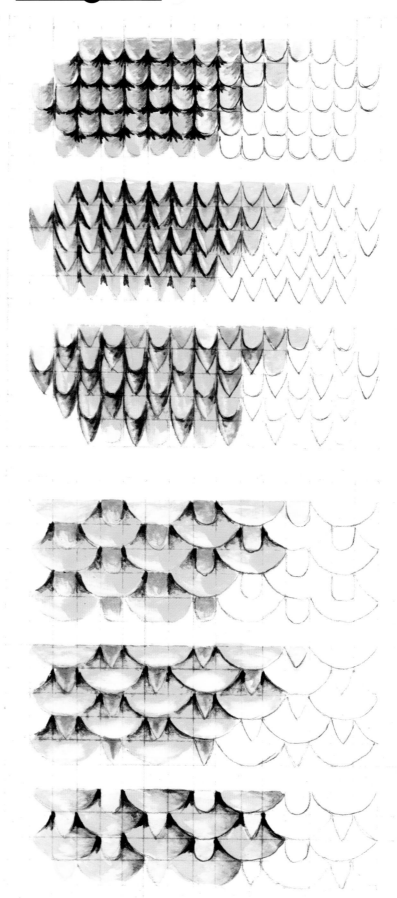

This dragon sports wide plating along his belly area. The plating is complemented by finer scales throughout the back and body regions. Note how both the scales and plates change size to accommodate their particular area of placement.

Creating
Test Patterns

OR How many dragons can I make from one design?

T he simplest way that I have found to experiment with these dragon patterns is to use a sheet of onion skin or parchment paper over the original design. In this way I can add ornamentation to different areas of the beast without having to rework the entire line drawing. Sail fins, manes, and horns can easily be penciled into place on the tracing paper and just as easily be erased or thrown away. When I am satisfied with the additions to the work, a second piece of tracing paper can be laid over the two and a final copy of the altered pattern made.

Artists who are familiar with the use of computers may want to scan the original drawings into the computer and then alter them in a computer-aided drawing program. Ornamentation, grid work for scales, and colors are quickly added, changed, and if need be, removed with these programs.

Let's begin with a very basic pattern of the Western Dragon. Perched on a name plate box, our sample (See Figure 8a.) has a typical long curling tail, simple bat wings, and a nicely arched neck. The belly area is obvious where it runs from under the head to the tip of the tail.

Adding the Guide Lines
Add some general guidelines for areas that might receive alterations. (See Figure 8b.) Sail fin guides are added along the top of the head, the back of the upper neck, the central

The sample dragon perches on a name plate box, just waiting for a few touches of detailing. The arched neck, long body, and curling tail will provide several areas to which ornamentation can easily be added.

Guidelines will be extremely helpful as you plan the changes you will be making to your dragon.

Dragon One
This dragon is ribbed throughout the length of its body. The fine ribbing on the back is complemented by heavier sections along the belly.

spine area, the upper tail area, and the tip of the tail. Each of these regions could have crests, hair, or horns. Add guidelines to the fins for reference when you begin the final sketch.

Once the sail guides are in place, pencil in your guidelines for the scaling or plating. Note how the scale guides roll with the body's tubular shape.

DRAGON ONE

For this sample, horns have been added along the upper edge of the bat wings, noting where the membrane will overlap the base of the horns. The body is ridged, similar to that of an earthworm. To the belly region has heavy octagon plating with a small rib between each section. The sides of the belly are accented with diamond-shaped scales.

Twin tentacles flow away from the upper brow and the back neck now has a finely serrated crest with radiating stays. The same style of cresting is placed at the tip of the tail. A small area of cresting has been applied beneath the eye area.

Note that this dragon has no back fin sails.

DRAGON TWO

This time the dragon's body is very finely scaled, almost to the point that it would have a smooth appear-

Dragon Two
Not all ornamentation needs to be exaggerated. For this dragon, the scaling is small, the sail fin is minimal, and the facial ornaments are kept close to the skull.

Dragon Three
This dragon will have a tiger's look when complete. The color stripes that will be added during the painting stage will be accented by the shadowing created by the belly scales.

ance but for the color changes in the scaling. The belly region is divided into three sections of ribbing, the central ribs are shown as small pieces interconnecting with the larger side ribs.

From the base of the neck to the beginning region of the tail our dragon now sports a small fluted back sail. The tail ends with a puff of sailing.

The face supports two horns that arch back toward the body, following the line of the upper skull. The eyes, the sides of his muzzle, and the lower jaw are heavily ridged or sectioned. A series of small horns has been added down the center of the muzzle. The final face change is the creation of a flowing beard that grows from the back of the lower jaw.

This dragon still has bat wings, but this time the leading edges of the sailings are serrated or tattered. There are even fine holes added to the inside areas of the wing membrane.

DRAGON THREE

Not every dragon needs to have scales, ribbing or fluting; some can have very smooth skin where color patterns are ideal. This is the case with the third dragon sample. By not texturing its back, this dragon can have striping added during the coloring phase. Armored plating is added to the belly, each plate overlapping the one

below it. This is a nice contrasting look for your dragon as you will have one area that is very smooth—the back—placed against one area that is heavily textured—the belly scales.

To carry the angular feeling of ornamentation throughout this beast the back sail fin has sharply pointed serration flowing away from the head and upper body. The serration becomes very distinct in the tail's sail. Finally, serrated sails have been placed at the sides of the back jaws and along the back of the neck. A mane of fine long hair flows from the dragon's forehead and jaw.

Heavy jointing has been added to the wing's stays and the membranes of the bat-style wings are now ridged or pleated.

DRAGON FOUR

Usually the ribbing or scaling on a dragon flows across the body, running from side to side. On this sample, the rib sections run from the back of the head to the tail tip. The belly is scaled with parallel rows of arrow heads ending at the tail tip with a large puff of fine flowing hair. This keeps the visual line flowing along the full length of the dragon's body.

The head also is adorned with areas of fine hair, along the forehead, back into the neck area, and beneath the chin as a beard. The horns for this dragon curl under

Dragon Four
It is important to carry the texture of the ornamentation throughout the beast. In this sample, the soft fine hair is complemented by the downy feathers on the wings.

Dragon Five
A very typical Western Dragon, this monster has definable scales, a ribbed belly and a pointed stinger at the tail tip.

much as a ram's horn would. Tusks have been added to the muzzle area.

Because the hair on this dragon's body yields a smooth texture, it seemed appropriate to keep that soft texturing in the wing structure. So, feathers are chosen for this dragon's wing covering.

DRAGON FIVE

The final dragon is much more typical to the common Western Dragon than the previous four samples. This beast has medium-sized fish scaling for its body texture and a ribbed belly. A small, folded section of body skin marks where the belly meets the back. The tail ends in a classic stinger point. A very small back sail is added, one that might only be extended into full position during flight or fights.

The head has a stiff serrated crest that runs from the tip of the muzzle to the back of the skull. Note that the scaling on the face is smaller, as is the scaling on the legs, to accommodate the tight areas of the body.

This dragon's wings are heavily serrated along the leading edges of the sails, to the point that each section becomes a small, individual wing unto itself.

Dragon Lore

8

OR Who are the most famous dragons of all time?

Virgin Hands

Lanivium, a small village, was protected by an aged dragon that dwelt in the depths of a cave. In exchange for guarding the village, the beast would demand his yearly allotment of food by hissing and twisting deep within the earth. Upon such occasions, a maiden was sent to pay the tribute to the fasting snake. Let down into the hole, this young girl, growing pale, with shaking hands, would thrust the tribute into the open mouth of the dragon. The beast snatched the delicacies from the maid, devouring tribute, basket, and all. Being sated, the beast would return to his slumber, granting the village protection for another year. If the tribute had been offered by virgin hands, the chaste would return to the surface to fall weeping into her parents loving arms and the village would know that the coming year would be bountiful. Unfortunately many young women never returned from the depths of the worm's abode. - Propertius (Sextus Aurelius Propertius), 1st Century B.C. Roman Poet.

Draco, the dragon that fills the night sky.

In the mythologies of Babylon, the king of the gods battled Draco, the representation of the primordial chaos that engulfed the universe. Upon slaying the beast, the God used the dragon's body to fashion the heavens. Draco can still be seen as a constellation in Ursa Minor.

Draco also appears in the legends of Minerva. During the time of wars between the giants and the gods, Draco fought with Minerva. She threw Draco's battered body into the heavens before it could recover from its wounds. The constellation Draco mimics a twisted snake winding among the neighboring stars.

Cadmus, a the founder of Thebes and a wise king, also fought and killed Draco. Having discovered that his faithful companions had been vanquished by this fearsome beast, Cadmus challenged the dragon, killing it with his spear. Upon the orders of Minerva, he then placed the teeth of the beast into the ground, and from this sowing, warriors appeared. Setting upon themselves, these warriors battle relentlessly until only five and Cadmus remained. It is said that these six men were the first people of the city of Thebes.

Hercules and the Hydra

Hercules is a well known mythological figure. In one story, Hercules had been sent by his brother Eurystheus to perform twelve labors in twelve years. Eurystheus' intent was to keep Hercules from claiming the throne that their mother Hera had given to Eurystheus. The Hydra was Hercules' Second Labor.

The Hydra had been bred in the swamps of Lerna and, having grown to maturity, had left the region to go out upon the plains, there raiding the properties and livestock of the local villagers. Hercules found the Hydra deep within a cave at Amynome and, having found him, forced him to leave the safety of his den by shooting flaming arrows into the entrance.

A beast of six heads appeared, each more terrible than the next, and each with the ability to regrow. Of these six heads, five were mortal and only the center head was immortal. The Hydra was not alone within its dwelling, as a huge crab lived among the coils. Throwing himself upon his challenger, the Hydra coiled its great length around Hercules feet, smothering the hero within the folds of its tremendous girth. As Hercules battled for his life he severed head after head with his blade only to discover that each head regrew two where one had been. As they battle the crab moved and darted, biting at Hercules's feet.

Realizing the dangers of the combat, Hercules killed the crab, then called for help from his cousin and charioteer, Iolaus. Iolaus set fire to a nearby grove of trees. Grasping a flaming branch, he scalded and caulderized each stump severed by Hercules, preventing those heads from regenerating. Only the immortal head of the Hydra still remained. Hercules severed this head and buried it under a stone beside the road. Hercules sliced open the Hydra's belly to dip his arrows into the deadly venom within.

Because Hercules had needed the help of Iolaus, Eurystheus refused to recognize the slaying of the Hydra as one of Hercules's labors.

The Lambton Worm

It would seem that the morning's sermon could not hold the attention of the young heir to the Lambtom kingdom, so John slipped out of the church to go fishing in the nearby River Wear. Having cast his line into the water, it quickly jerked and John struggled valiantly to pull the tremendous catch to the bank. What he found at the end of the line shocked poor John. Black skinned with a dragon's head, this three foot long Worm was indeed repulsive. Not wishing to return the beast to the waters and not wishing to take it home, he threw the worm into a nearby well where it fell into the depths.

John was shaken by this adventure for he saw himself in the Worm. All of the ugly deeds and many wrongs he had created throughout his short life haunted him. He chose to correct his ways and redeem his terrible deeds by taking upon himself a pilgrimage to the Holy Lands. So the Lambton heir left his home and traveled aboard.

Little did John know that the Worm had survived the well and had grown to vast proportions. While John was away from his kingdom, the Worm had left the well and taken up residence near the town. The Worm had become so large that it was said to be able to wrap its length around the Lambton Hill nine times. This beast fed its girth on the villager's cattle and livestock, even taking an occasional townsman. In a desperate attempt to satis-

fy the dragon, the village offered the beast milk, a legendary pacifier to dragonkind. Twenty gallons where placed each day into a large trough and, having drank the offering, the Worm sluggishly crept back to the hill to sleep. Still the villagers could find no way to rid themselves of this gigantic serpent.

Upon his return and learning of the great Worm's existence, John knew he would have to confront the monster. Seeking the advice of a local witch, he had a special suit of armor created by the blacksmith, one that had sharp blades and spikes mounted across the breast plate. As he left the witche's home, she warned him that should he kill the Worm he must also kill the next living thing he saw or a terrible curse would fall upon those who carried the Lambton name.

The Worm was quite aware of the approaching figure, for even as John raised his sword to wield its blade upon the beast, the monster jumped, wrapping its coils around the man. Tightening its hold, the Worm put all its strength into crushing the captured man, yet this very act caused the blades and spikes of John's armor to slice the beast's body and it fell to the ground in many pieces. The worm was finally dead.

Returning home from this great battle John came upon his father in the road. Realizing that he, his own sire, was the first living creature that John has seen since killing the beast, John could not follow the second part of the advice from the witch. Instead, hoping to somehow satisfy the prophecy, John slew his favorite dog. This, however, did not prevent the curse. After that day all that carried the Lambton name were cursed to die far away from the peace and safety of their home.

Indian Worms

Ancient legends from India imply that the Worm was large enough to swallow both stags and bulls whole. In fact, the Worms were so tremendous that they took to hunting elephants. Waiting in hiding near a watering hole, the Worm would lunge toward the unsuspecting elephant, wrap its tail around the animal and squeeze the elephant into exhaustion. Then the dragon would bite into the elephant's throat, draining it of all its blood. This created a great problem for the locals because it seemed that the elephant's blood was an intoxicant to the dragon and drunken dragons are very dangerous creatures.

Hunting elephants was not always a successful pastime for the Indian dragon, for it seems that if the dragon was not careful, the exhausted elephant could fall upon the dragon crushing the dragon's belly. Therefore, it was common that a traveler would stumble upon a dragon wrapped tightly around an elephant's body, both dead from the encounter.

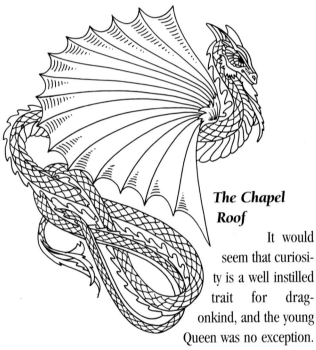

The Chapel Roof

It would seem that curiosity is a well instilled trait for dragonkind, and the young Queen was no exception. Since her hatching she had become fascinated with the strange community of creatures that lived at the base of her hill. Each day she would lie upon the stony shelf to her cliff and watch their constant comings and goings along the old road. Always she wondered where they were going in such a hurry and what they might be doing once they got wherever it was they were headed.

After quite a time her curiosity became too strong to be denied and so the queen dragon changed her shape, taking the form of one of the human females. Her hind limbs grew into long slender legs, her wings became flowing robes to cover her form, and her mane grew into hair of copper red that fell to the middle of her back. So disguised, the young Queen ventured off to explore the creatures' village.

Upon entering the village, she was met by a tall, dark-haired man. The man was quite taken by the young woman that approached him. Never had he seen so beautiful a lady. She, too, was entranced by the handsomeness of this human that stood watching her. It came to pass that she spent the afternoon with him as he showed her each site of the town. At sunset the young Queen extended her gratitudes to the gentleman for his courtesies and slipped away to return to her home and her dragon form.

Within a few days she again became curious. What was the man doing today? Would he be at the village, might he be waiting there to see if she returned? She had learned that he was called the King, what could this mean? Unable to silence her inquisitiveness, the Queen once again took the shape of a human woman and headed to visit the town. The King was there, indeed waiting in the town in hopes that beautiful woman would once again appeared.

Over the next few months she returned often to the town to visit the King. The King, as Kings will do, courted the young woman and one day asked if she would become his wife. Through the many visits, she had come to love his gentle spirit and respect the depth of his wisdom, so the young Queen agreed. Soon they were married and the town's people were delighted, for they too had fallen in love with this wonderful young woman.

As the years passed, the love between the King and Queen grew. They were blessed with several strong sons and a daughter. The town prospered under their guidance and the people cherished their beautiful Queen. Everything was wonderful, well, almost everything. It seemed that the Queen has one small habit that left the King very perplexed. Every Sabbath the King, Queen, and their children would dress in their finest clothes and attend the mass at the local chapel. Every Sabbath the family would sit in the front pew to listen to the sermons given by the priest, and every Sabbath just as the Sacramental Communion was to be given the young Queen would quietly rise and disappear from the church.

When returning home the King would question his wife, "Why do you leave the church?" She never gave him an answer. Over the years, this began to prey on the King's mind, and finally, he devised a scheme to confront his wife and discover the reasons that she did not participate in this most Holy ritual.

The next Sabbath, the family entered the chapel and took their seats in the front pew. The priest launched into his sermon and having finished began the preparations for the Communion. At this point, the Queen quietly rose from her seat and slipped to the chapel doors. There she found the doors blocked by the King's guard. Turning to escape through the front of the chapel, the Queen was again blocked by guards that refused to let her pass. Knowing that she was trapped, the young Queen lost her human form and the King watched in horror as a Red Dragon emerged and burst through the rafters of the chapel. The Queen was never seen again.

The Ladon Serpent

The Hydra was not the only dragon that Hercules faced. The Ladon Serpent is the second beast of the eleventh labor. This monster was said to be a half mile long with a mouth that extended from the tip of its nose to the tip of its tail. This huge mouth was filled with razor-like teeth the size of elephant tusks. This dragon, so much more fearsome than the Hydra, made Hercules hesitate to approach. He needed some scheme whereas he could destroy the animal from a distance.

Hercules found an old dead tree that contained a large bee hive. Breaking the hive from the tree he threw branch, bees, and all into the open mouth of the Ladon Serpent. The bees, angry at this disturbance stung the beast within his mouth and throat, thus killing the creature.

Siegfried, Regin, and Fafnir

Now it was Regin, the dwarf, that told Siegfried of the great dragon hoard that could bring him power and fame, for Regin knew of a beast named Fafnir that guarded just such a treasure. This interested Siegfried, and taking up his father's sword that had recently been reforged, he and the dwarf set out to find the beast.

Regin had not told Siegfried all of the tale. He had kept to himself the fact that his brother, Fafnir, had murdered their father. Upon his death Fafnir had taken the wealth of the kingdom that had been his sire's. Being so greedy and fearful that another might take his treasure, Fafnir turned himself into a dragon to protect this golden hoard.

Now Siegfried and Regin knew that it was near impossible to kill a dragon because its hide was so tough and scaly that no blade could broach it. So Regin proposed digging a pit just outside the dragon's cave. Having done so, Siegfried hid within the pit and Regin piled branches over the opening. He waited for hours deep within the earthen hole for the animal to pass on its daily trip to the watering hole.

A great shadow appeared darkening the pit. Siegfried taking his sword in both hands shoved it upward through the branch covering and in to the underbelly of the monster. The dragon having been struck in its one tender area fell to the ground.

Regin, seeing the great beast dead took his knife and carved out the dragon's heart. This he roasted and offered to share with Siegfried. But on handing his companion a piece of the prized meat, Regin burnt his hand. As the dwarf sat by the fire, sucking his scorched fingers, he heard a chattering in the trees above. The ravens were talking, saying that Regin now planned to kill Siegfried and keep the treasure for himself. Siegfried once again took up his father's sword and sliced the head from Regin. It was Siegfried who claimed the golden hoard in the end.

The great king shouted to the dragon, bidding him to come and fight. The beast charged the king, belching noxious fumes. Raising his shield, Beowulf rushed to the dragon through the terrible flames, yet upon drawing his sword the blade broke. Even as Beowulf reached for his dagger, the dragon bite him.

Wiglaf, unable to stand aside any longer, rushed to the King and taking up his sword plunged it into the underside of the dragon's jaw. The amazement of being wounded startled the monster, causing him to let go of his death grip upon Beowulf. The king and his faithful companion were then able to take their blades against the beast until the dragon collapsed.

The king lie upon the ground, the deadly venom seeping though his body. Wiglaf in hopes of reviving Beowulf held up an arm full of treasure. Yet the king knew that this was his last day. Taking his helmet and ring, Beowulf, in his last act of life, made Wiglaf the King of the Great in his stead.

St. George and the Dragon

Upon King Ulther's death, he was buried as befits a ruler of his great stature on a bed of gold, the wealth of his kingdom. This bed of treasure was so great that the tomb smelled of silver, gold and jewels, the very likes of which attracted a most fearsome beast. The dragon, as dragons will do, settled himself upon the tomb claiming the hoard as his own.

This dragon was huge with an appetite to match and soon had ravaged the country side to fill its empty belly. Hoping to some how control this terrible situation, the new King decreed that the best of the sheep flock should be brought to the dragon each morning. Soon all of the sheep within the village were consumed. The sheep were gone, yet the King still had a hungry dragon on his lands, so he ordered that the cattle should now be offered. These, too, went to fill the belly of the beast as did every living animal that the village had.

With no more livestock to offer this monster, the King came to a hard decision and made a decree that there should be a lottery of all the virgin women within the town. From the lottery, each morning one woman's name would be drawn and sent to the beast so the rest of the village would be safe. Each day, another name was taken from the basket and each day one more girl faced

Beowulf and Fire Dragon

One of Beowulf's servants was in trouble, and to hide from his misdeeds, he ran from the town. Coming upon a cave, he slipped inside to discover a dragon's hoard of gold buried deep beneath the earth. Seeing the riches piled before him, the servant decided that perhaps a golden goblet would buy away the troubles he had created. So he took the goblet and returned to the town.

Late that night, the dragon awoke and, upon checking his hoard, quickly found that his golden goblet was gone. In fury, the dragon charged from his hiding hole and swept down upon the sleeping town. With his great breath, he set the village on fire.

Beowulf, having seen the destruction of his kingdom, gathered a small band of brave warriors and set off to find this beast and put an end to its life. Within the band was Wiglaf who was greatly concerned for his king. He knew that this great man, though very old, was determined to face the monster single handed. Wiglaf begged Beowulf to allow him to stand by his side when it came time to challenge the fire dragon. For all of his begging, Beowulf refused Wiglaf and went to the cave entrance alone.

the monster. Each day all the remaining names were returned to the basket. So a terrible cloud of despair settled upon the small kingdom.

As it would happen, the King had a young daughter and soon it was her name that was pulled from the basket. The King felt terrible guilt because there was no way that he could save her, it being unjust that his subjects' children must become food for the beast but not his own. The King's daughter had recently come to the true church and so prayed every day that the lottery was drawn that her new faith would sustain her. She chose not to take the answer that many of the young girls in the village found to have their names removed from the basket. Instead, she remained chaste and pure as her faith decreed she should.

The entire village mourned that morning as the beloved princess was taken to Dragon's Hill and chained to the feeding post. With great composure, the girl allowed herself to be chained and waited alone and in silence for the dragon to awaken. The guards withdrew not having the courage to watch this young woman devoured. As the monster crept from its hole its fearsome countenance turned to gaze upon his meal. Even for a princess, this beast was too much to bear. The morning stillness was broken with her shrieks of terror.

Again, as it would happen in such tales, there was a young knight on the road that morning who heard these cries of fear. The gentleman had been one of the Imperial Guard of the old Emperor, but upon Ulster's death the guard had disbanded. So looking for some new adventure, the Knight was traveling through the countryside. Even as this brave man urged his steed up the hill toward the princess, the dragon had taken notice of the young and tender feast set before him. His nostrils filled with noxious fumes nuzzled the sweet morsel with interest. The poor princess, overcome by his foul breath, fell faint.

Just as the beast was about the devour the fair woman, the Knight charged the dragon hurling his spear at the dragon's exposed hindquarters. Crying in pain, the dragon turned. Sword drawn, the Knight charged against the dragon, wing and shield intertwined in combat. Knocked from his horse by the claw, the Knight gallantly battled on against the great monster, blade against tooth.

The noise of the battle was so great that the people

of the village dared the dragon's hill to discover the causes of this tremendous clattering and howling. They watched in amazement as the Knight's blade created slice after slice in the dragon's bulk, it's acidic blood pouring to the ground where it burnt the very earth. Finally the air was filled with an anguished howl as the dragon lay down to death.

Rushing forward with joy, the people took up the hero and freed their princess. Taking both to the castle, they were greeted by a King overcome with relief, for now his daughter was safely returned and his kingdom saved from the ravages of the monster. As the reward for his heroism, the King gave the young Knight his daughter's hand in marriage so that he would one day inherit the throne of the kingdom.

The dragon was buried next to Ulster on Dragon's Hill and there the people of the town carved a great likeness to the beast into the chalk that to this day would always be remembered.

The Yorkshire Dragon

The Yorkshire dragon that lay upon Loschy Hill was said to have the deadliest of tongues, covered with venomous slime. Its mouth was full of fine, sharp teeth the size of pitchfork prongs. It came to pass that Peter Loschy should come upon the dragon and so set to combat with the beast. As he hacked upon the dragon's tongue, he was able to slice great pieces from its tip. Each piece fell to the ground where Peter's loving and faithful dog took the pieces into his jaws and carried them off to the river.

With the task done and the dragon dead at Peter's feet, the hound, so pleased with his master for such a great accomplishment, licked the knight's face in praise. Unbeknownst to the brave dog, the poison from the dragon's tongue now covered the face of his master. Together Peter and his devoted companion lay down next to the dragon and died.

Dragon
Patterns

9

Craft patterns are a starting point for the artist. With the designs in this section you can begin creating your own unique dragon beasts. Each pattern is made so that it can be used as is or easily altered to fit your needs and media requirements.

So as you browse through these ideas, note on each pattern those areas that can quickly be adapted. Remember that tails can be lengthened and stretched, mouths can be opened to accommodate fire and ice breath, wings can be expanded or reduced, anything goes with dragon work. You can mix and match the patterns using the wings from one beast and the body of another.

For the woodcrafter, there are designs that include architectural supports and acanthus leaves, however, the oil artist may wish to lift only he dragon from the design. Many designs shown here are full bodied or facial portraits. These can be added to a scene of your own making to create a story.

It is hoped that you will discover many ideas and new patterns for your fine ar and craft work.

Parental Devotion

Sentinel

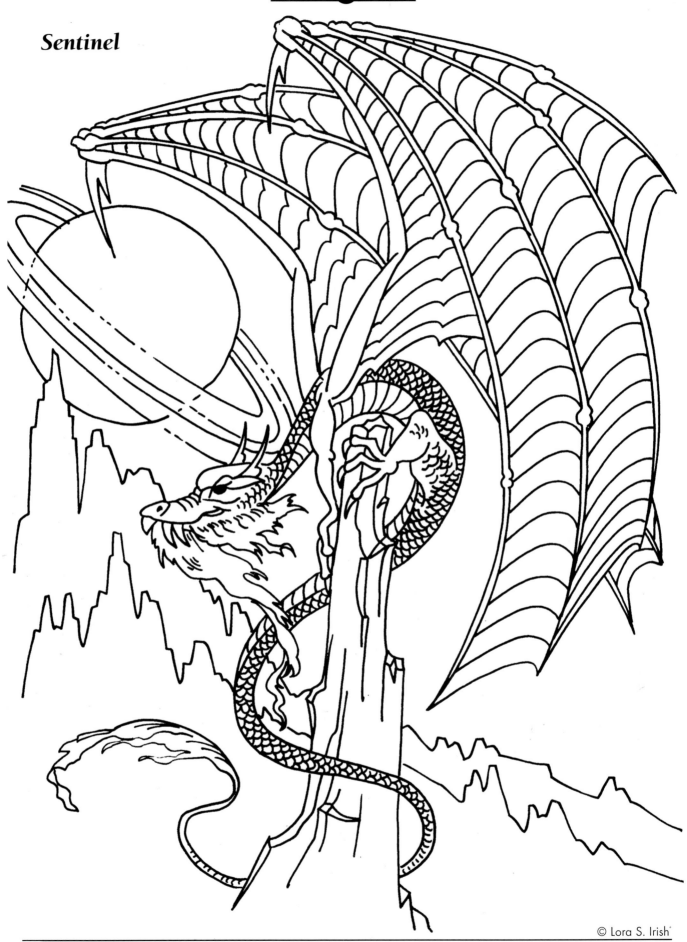

© Lora S. Irish

Fire Heights

New Born Fury

Golden Bed

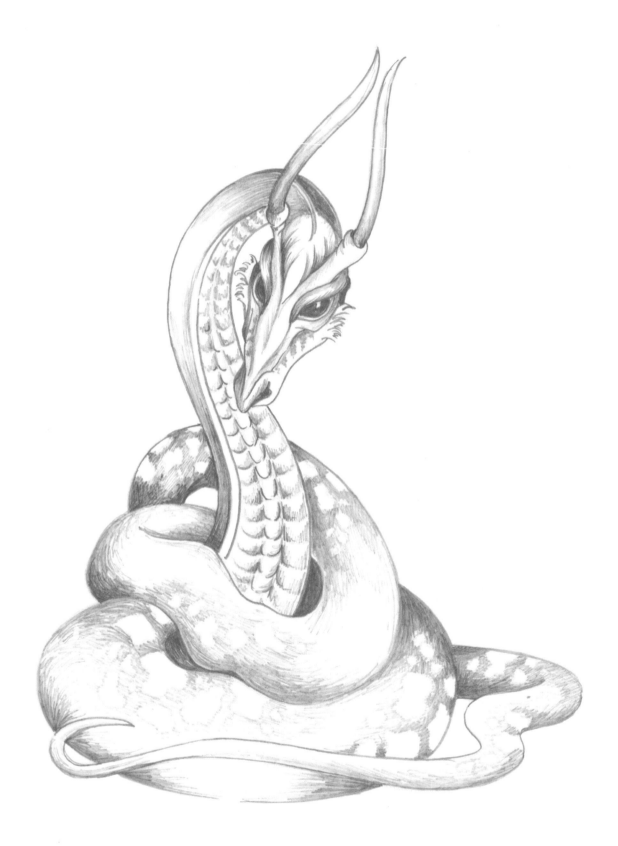

Lambton Worm

Towering Monarch

Ocean Crests

Three-Toed Adversary

Triple Challenge

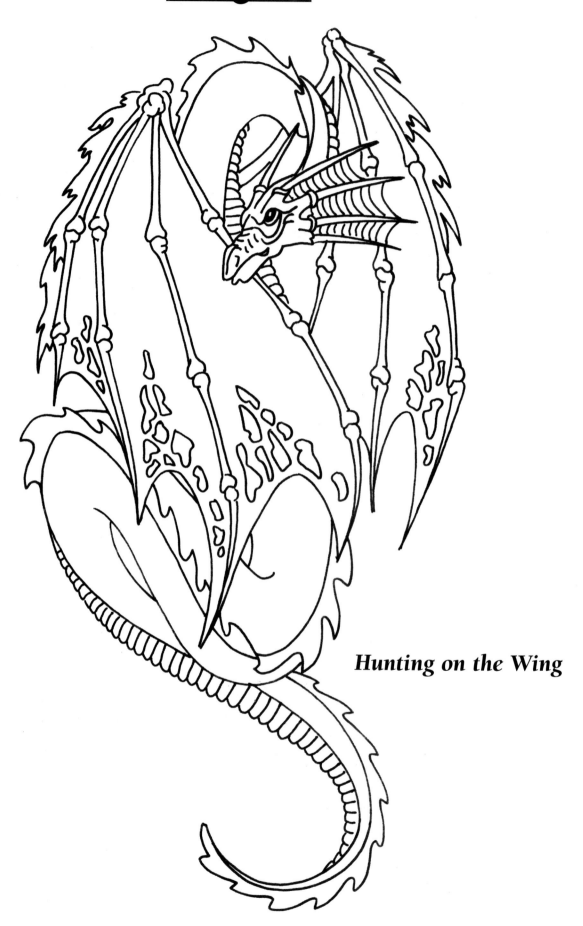

Hunting on the Wing

Architectural Overseer

Dangerous Curves

Toadstool Heights

Double-Horned Monarch

Mexican Feathered Lizard

Mushroom Fairy Dragon

Ribbed-Back Sample Dragon

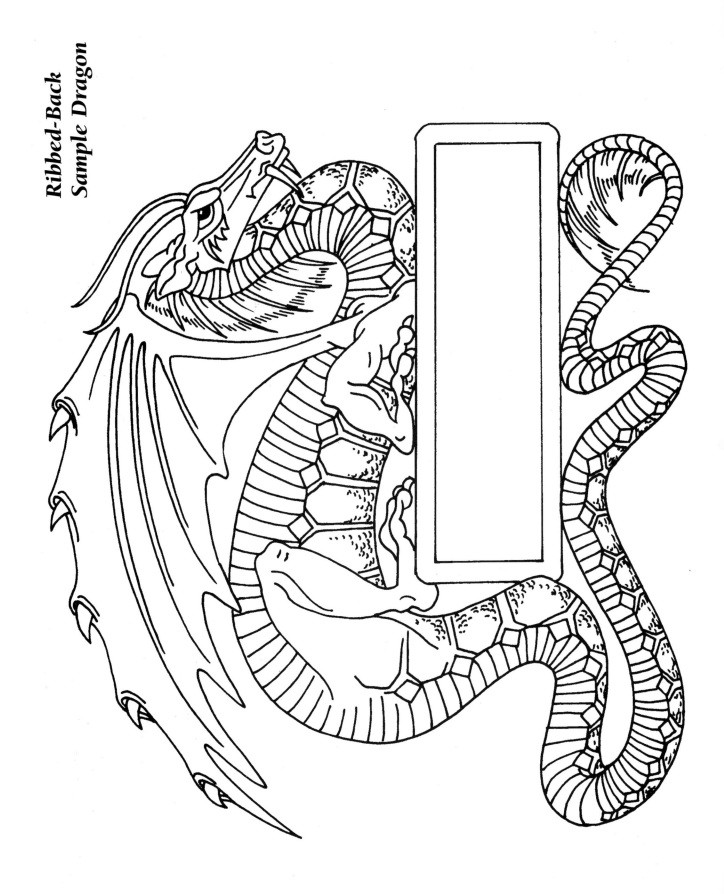

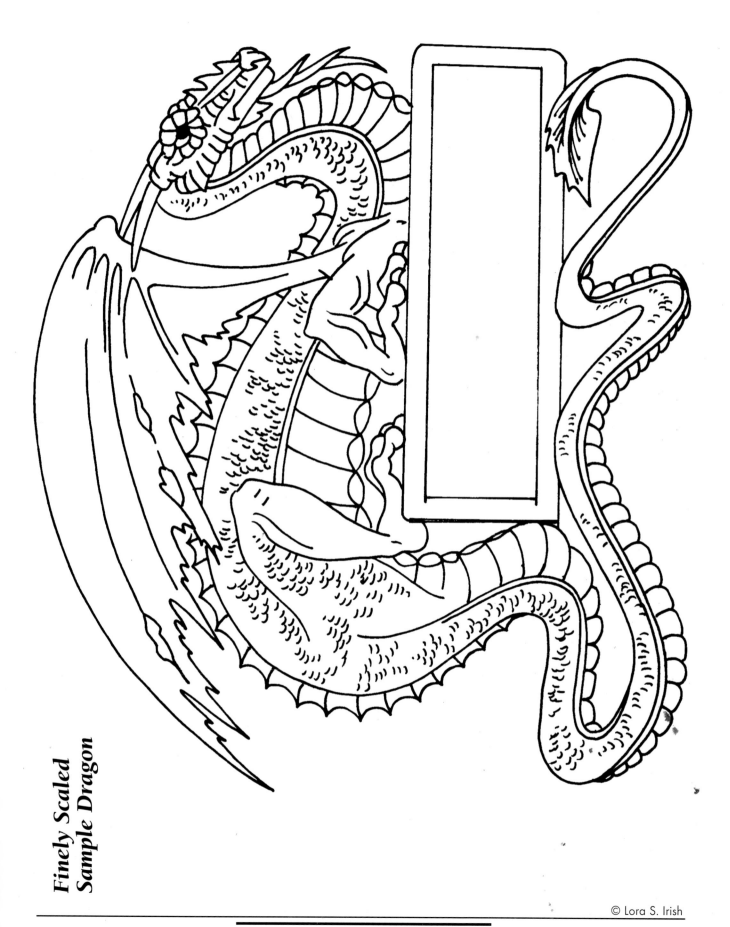

Finely Scaled
Sample Dragon

**Ram's Horn
Sample Dragon**

Striped and Bearded Sample Dragon

**Crested Orbs
Sample Dragon**

Lizard Perch

Celtic Cross Dragons

Architectural Sea Dragon

Split Personality

Bat-Winged Worm

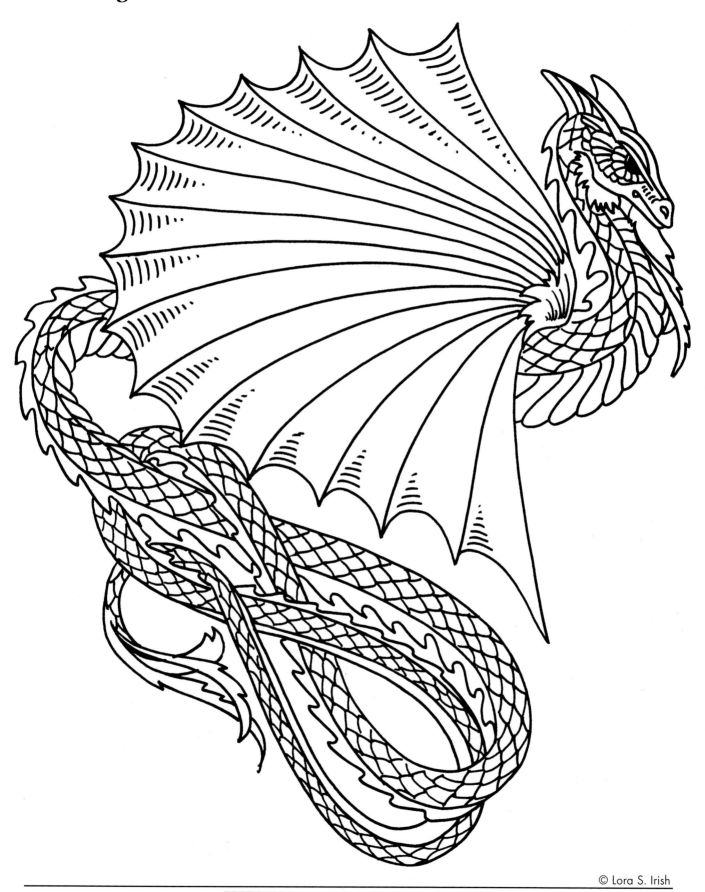

Dragon Curl

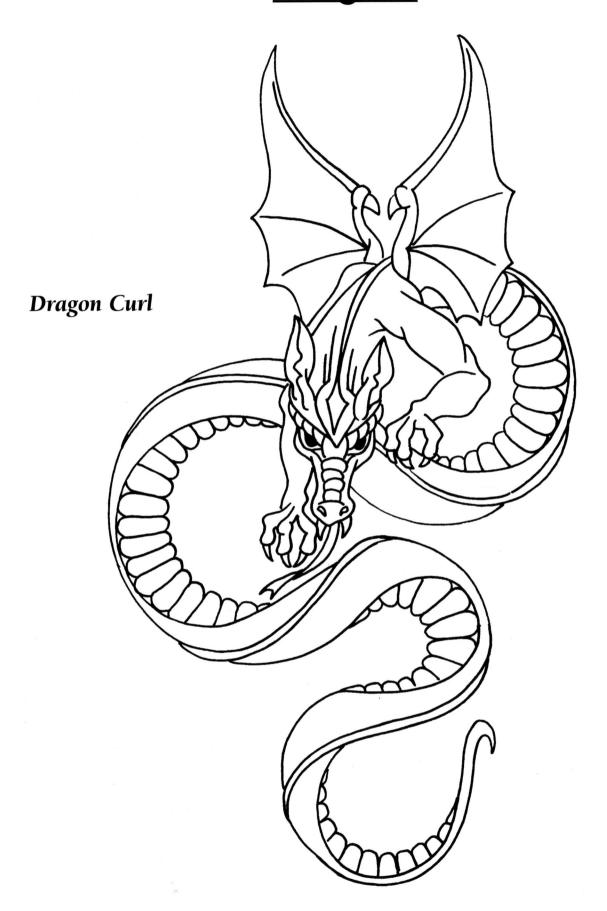

Poised for Battle

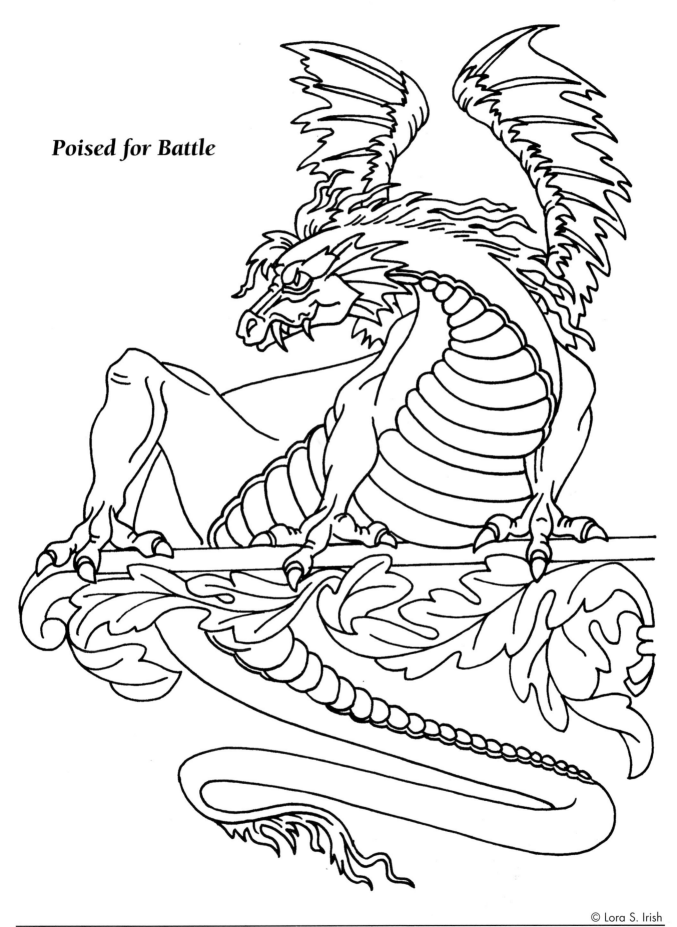

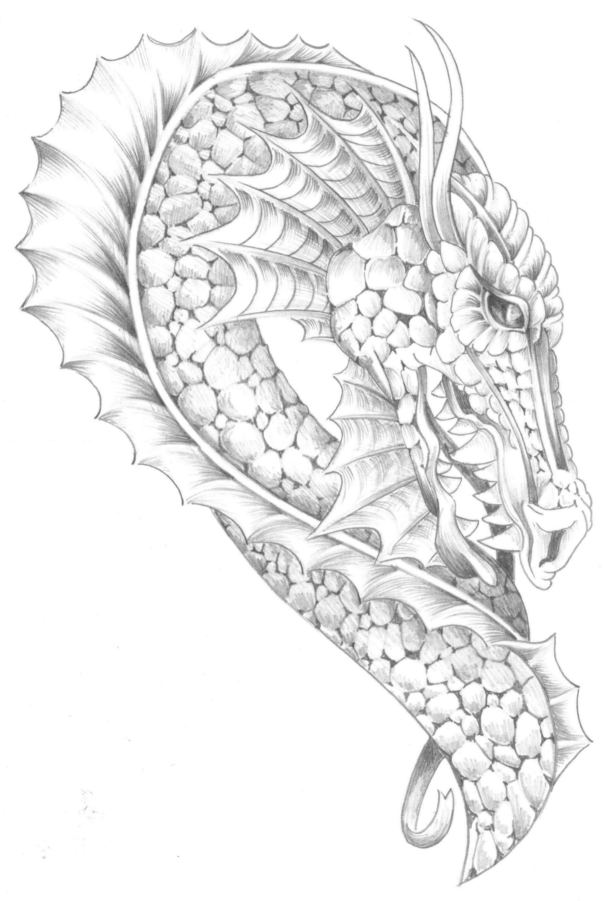

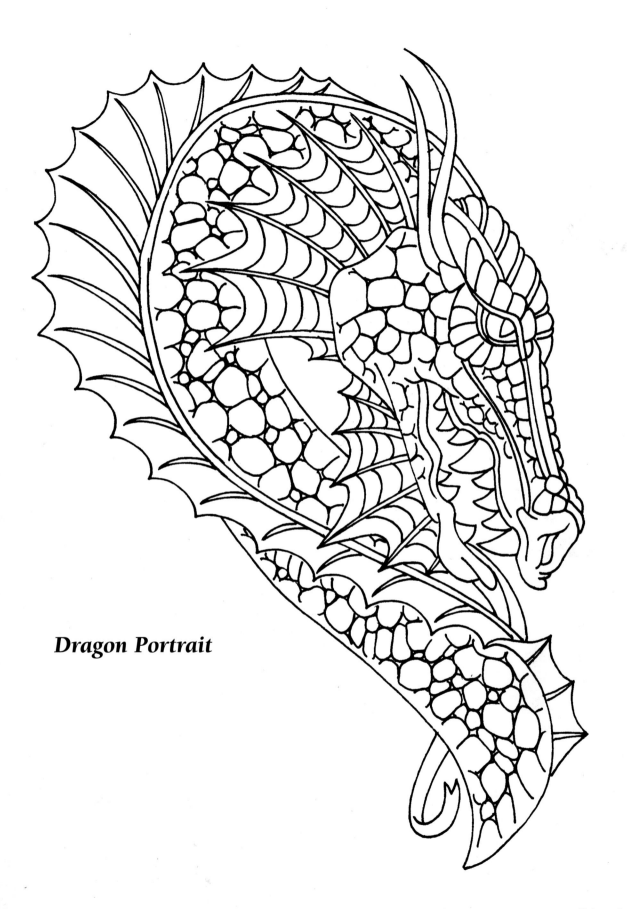

Dragon Portrait

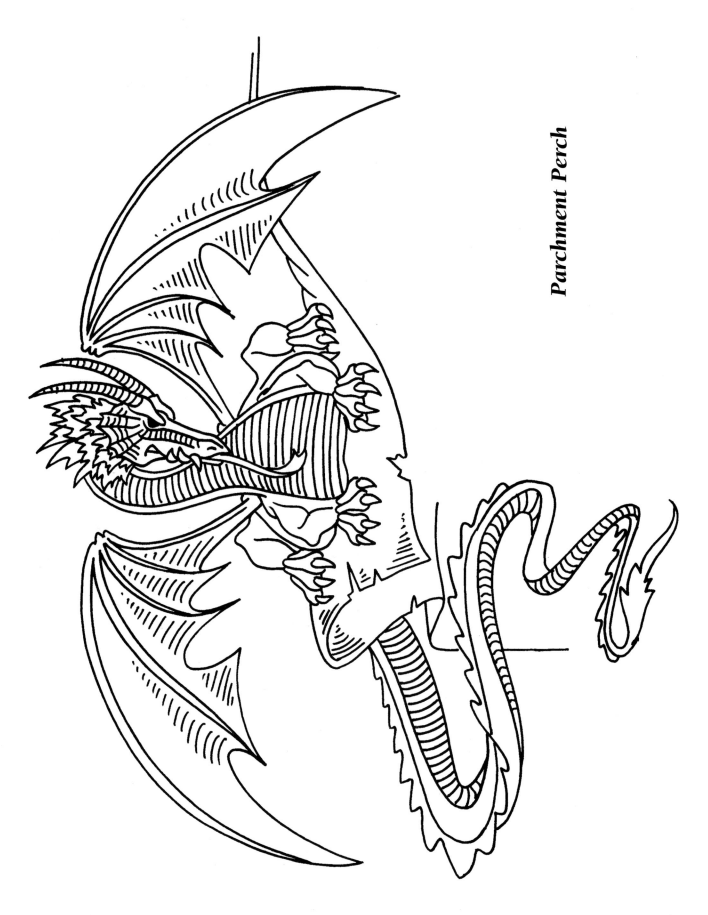

Parchment Perch

**Coiling Wyvern
Shield and Sword**

Wyvern Mirror

Bearded Demon

On the Prowl

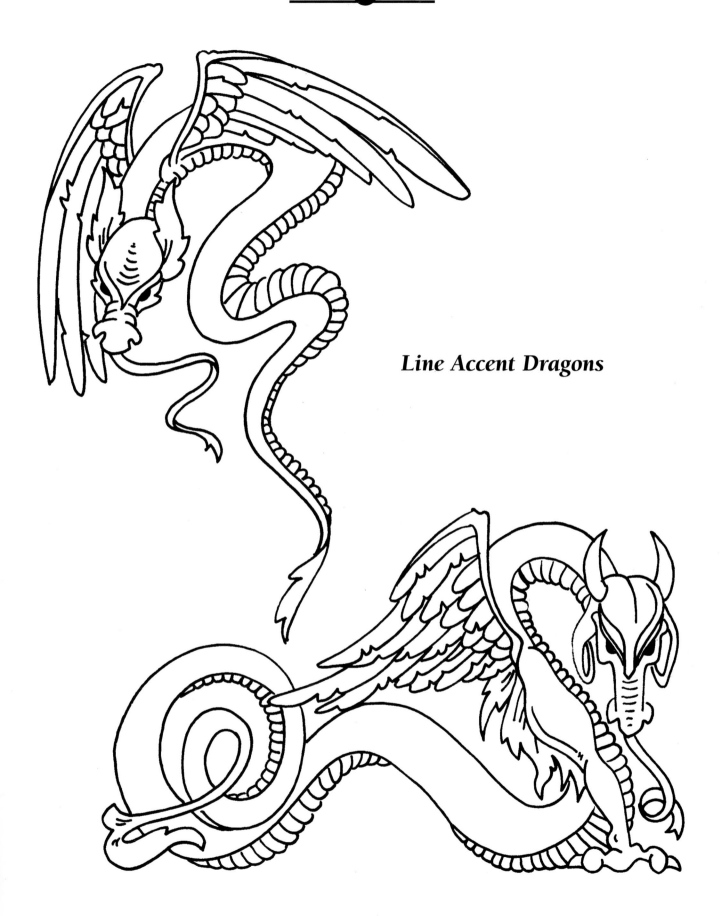

Line Accent Dragons

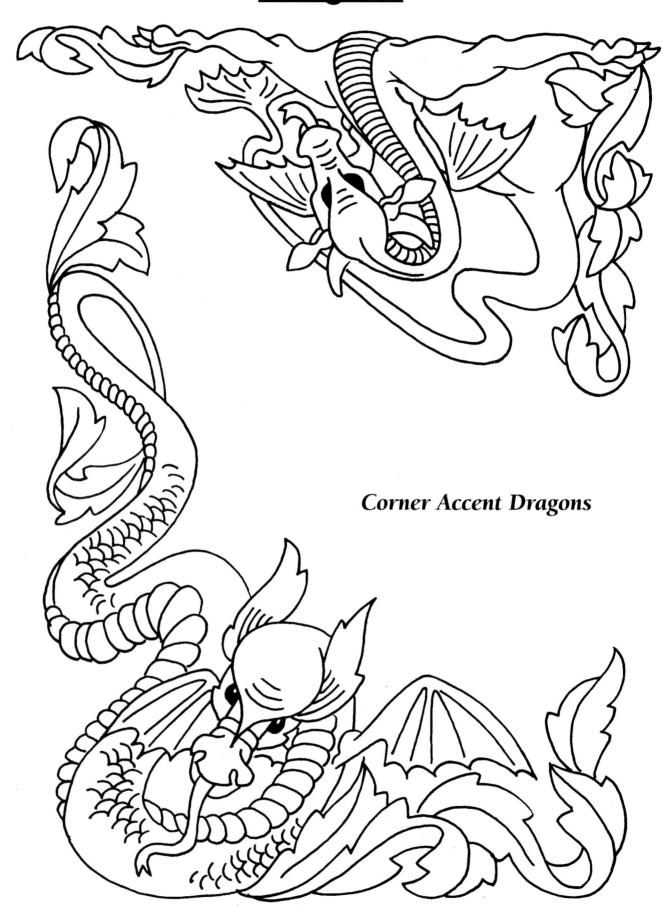

Corner Accent Dragons

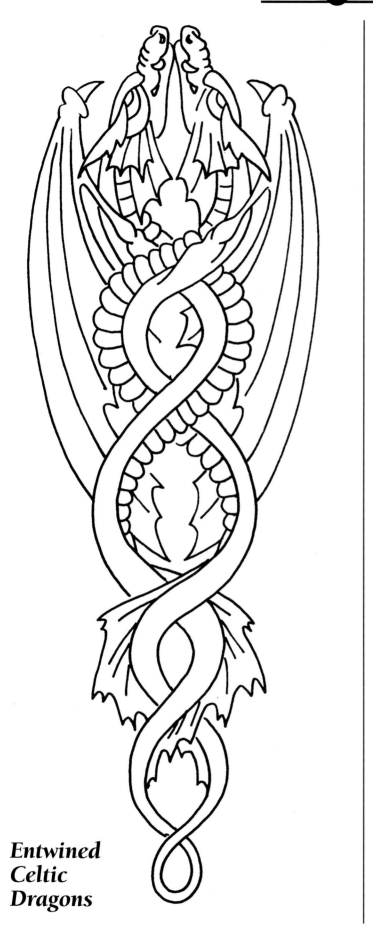

Entwined Celtic Dragons

Curved Lindworm Accent

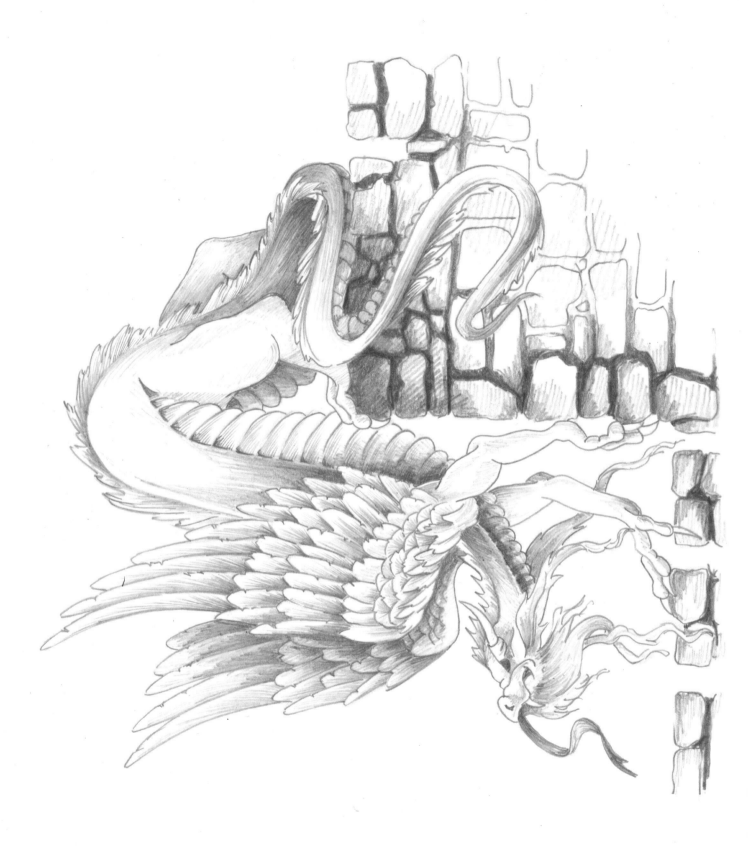

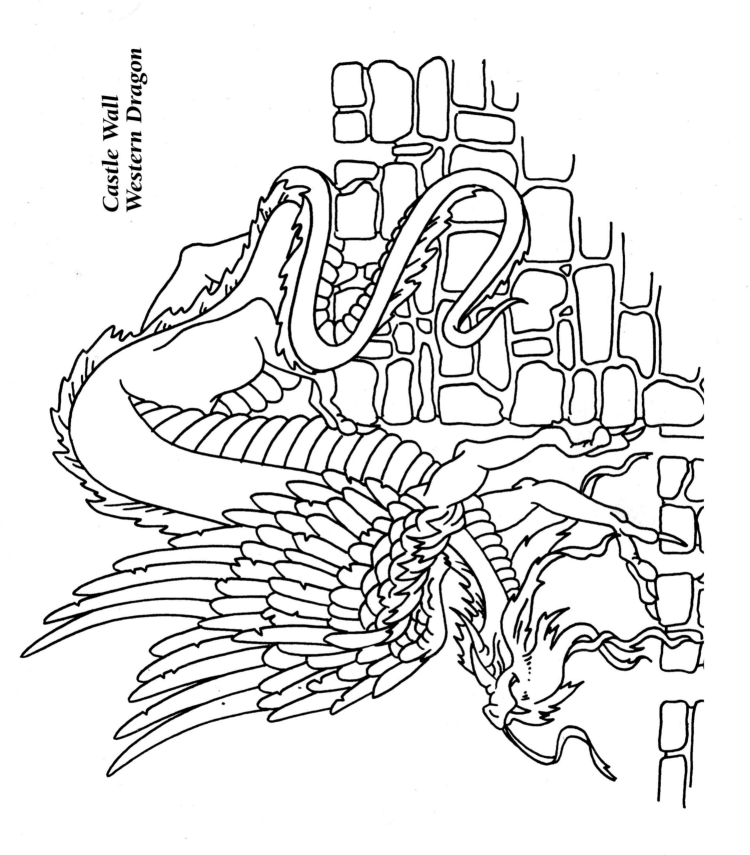

Castle Wall
Western Dragon

Battle-Ready Western

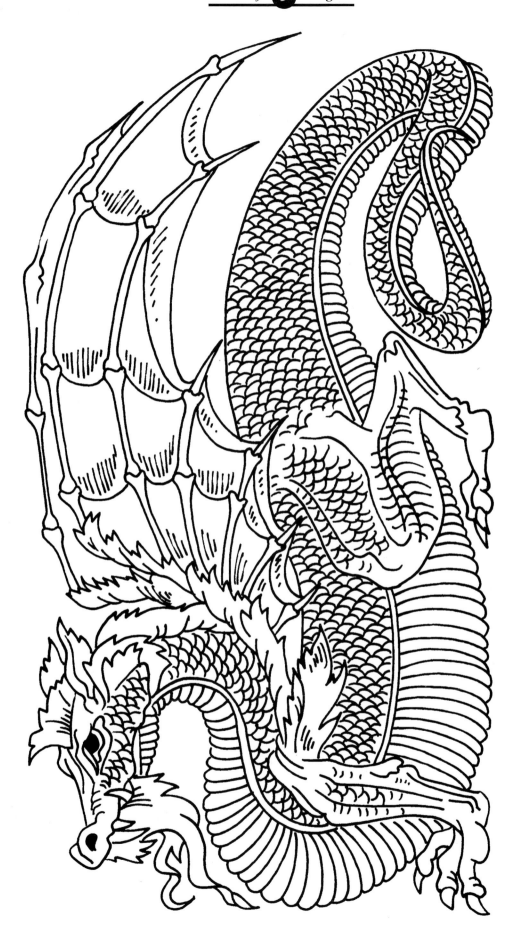

Classic Western Dragon

Eagle Claws Portrait

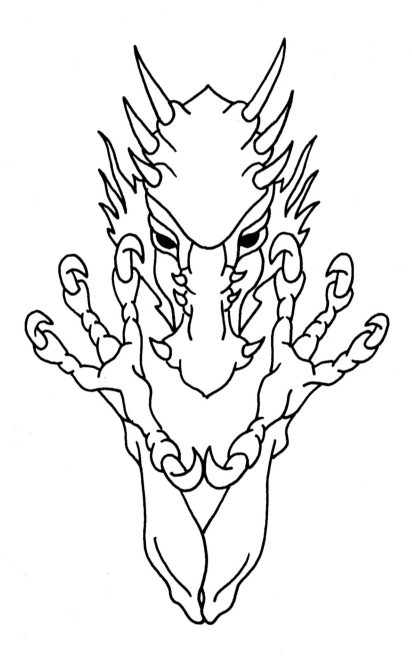

Western Rapier Dragon

Winged Snake Shield

Cliff-Side Throne

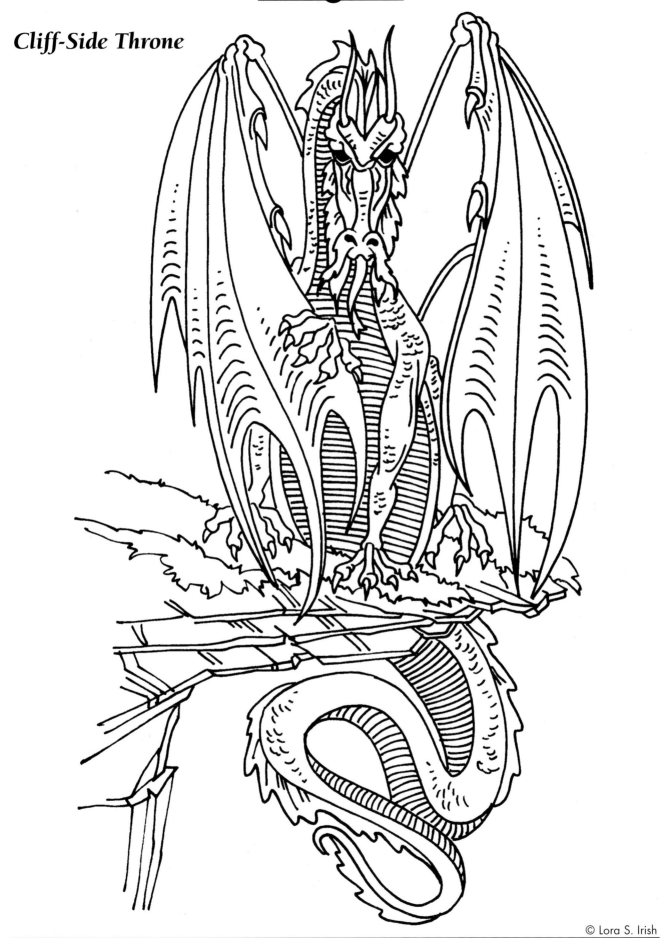

High-Winged Western

Wyvern Orb Mirror Image

Little Angel

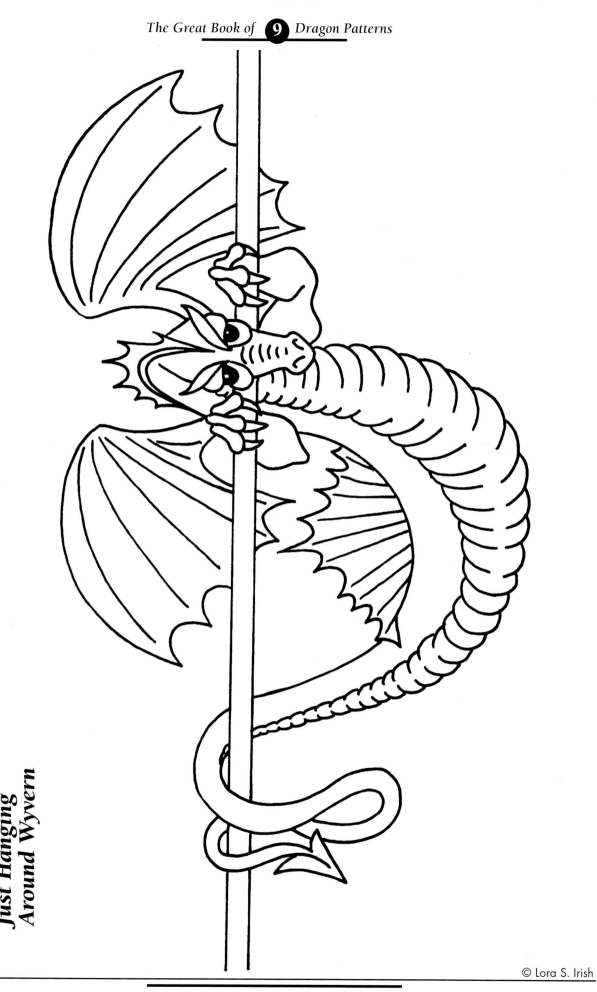

Just Hanging Around Wyvern

Afternoon Nap

Devoted Heart Portrait

Young Fairy Love

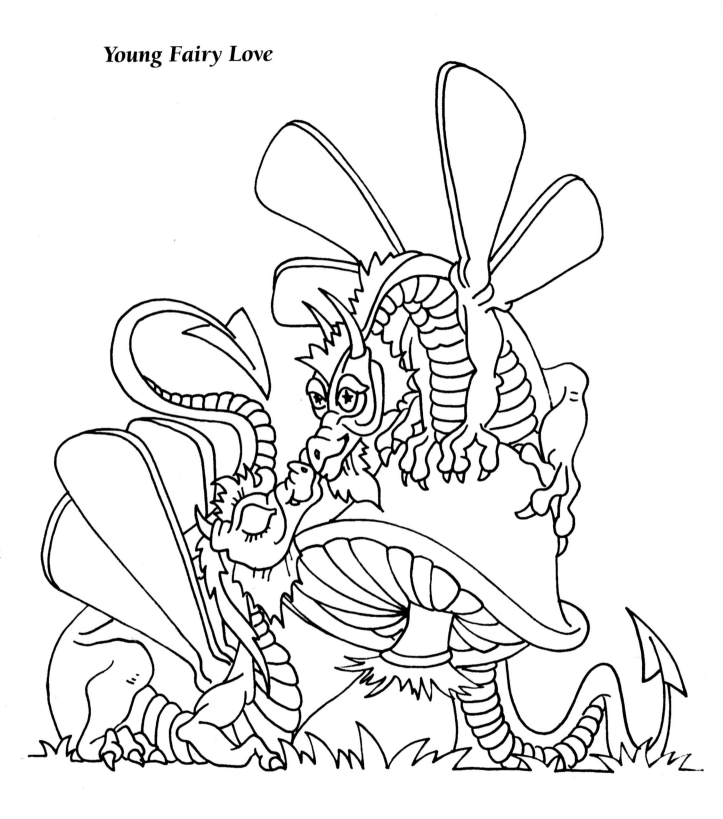

Peek-A-Boo Western

Encircling the Heavens

Stylized Feather Dragon

Dagger Wrap Worm

Feathered Wing Serpent

Celtic Corner Serpent

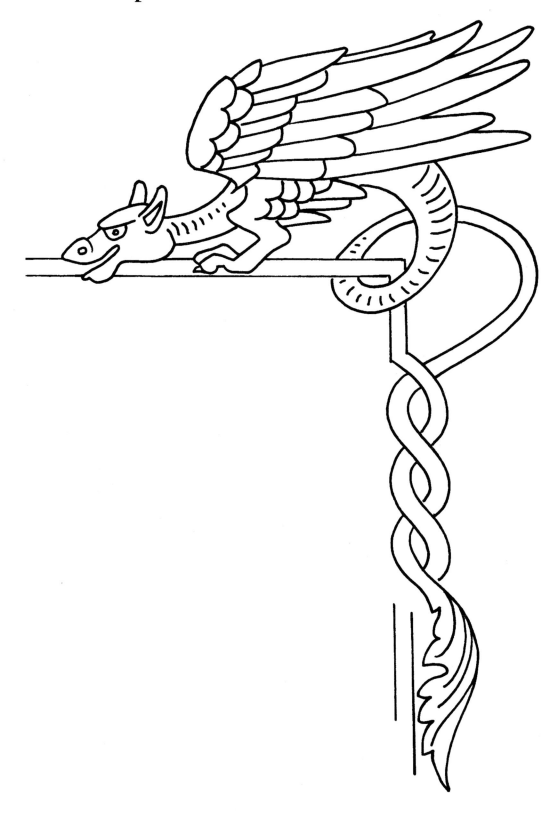

Twin Demon Shield

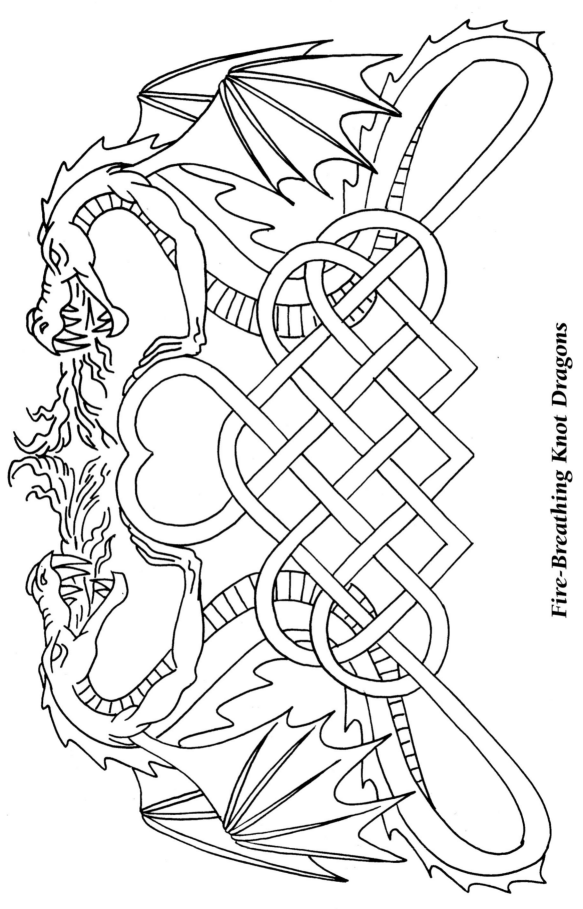

Fire-Breathing Knot Dragons

Entwined Tail Knots

Full-Faced Heraldry Accent

Profiled Heraldry Accent

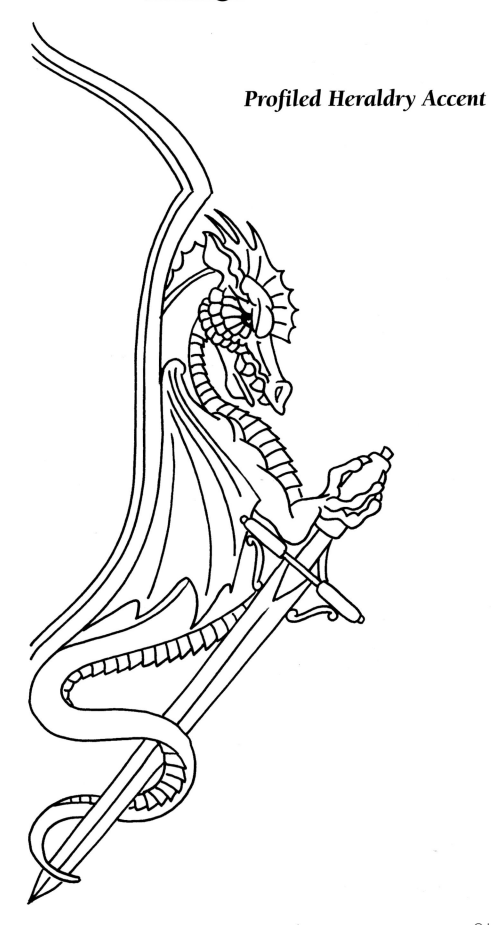

Saxon Dragon Shield

Panel Winged Serpent

Heart Dragon Mirror Image

Wyvern Arch

Horned Beast Portrait

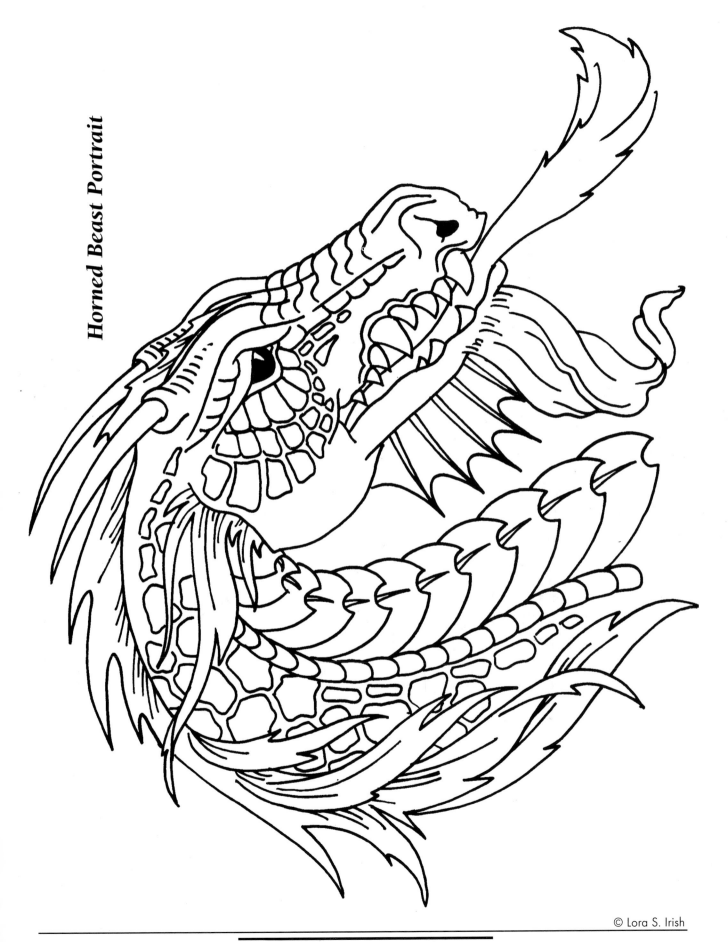

Proudly Perched Western

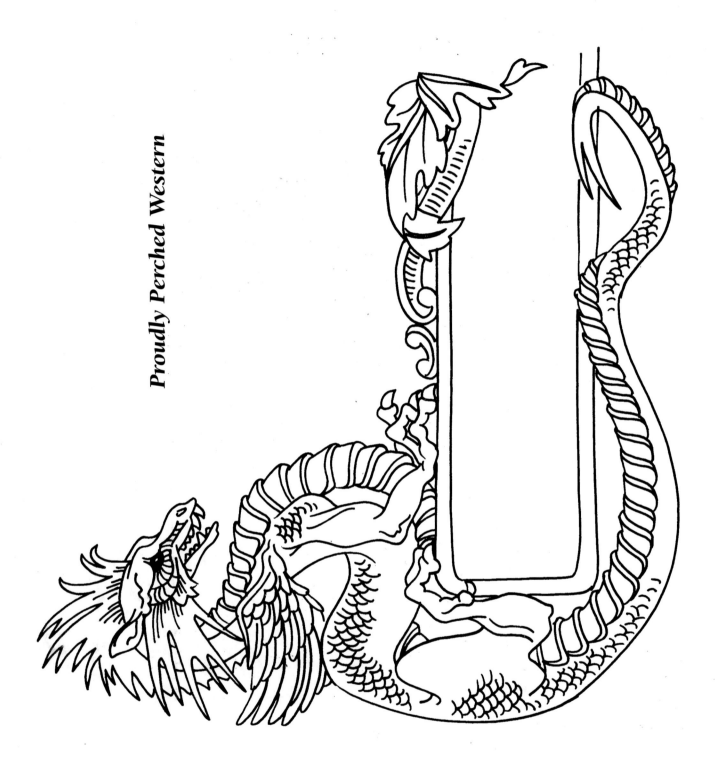